ROAST GRIND BREW SERVE REPEAT

SCOTTISH
INDEPENDENT
COFFEE
GUIDE

Nº1

Salt Media, 5 Cross Street, Devon, EX31 1BA.
www.saltmedia.co.uk
Tel: 01271 859299
Email: ideas@saltmedia.co.uk

Salt Media Indy Coffee Guide team:
Marcus Chapman, Nick Cooper,
Catherine Jones, Kathryn Lewis,
Tamsin Powell, Jo Rees, Chris Sheppard,
Dale Stiling and Mark Tibbles.
Design and illustration: Salt Media

A big thank you to the *Indy Coffee Guide*
committee (meet them on page 126)
for their expertise and enthusiasm, **our
headline sponsors** Schluter and Cimbali,
and sponsors Beyond the Bean, Bunn and
Yeo Valley. **Thanks to** Jamie Treby **and
special thanks to photographer**
Gavin Smart for his work on the guide.

Coffee shops, cafes and roasters are
invited to be included in the guide based
on meeting criteria set by our committee,
which includes a high quality coffee
experience for visitors, use of UK roasted
beans and being independently run.

www.indycoffee.guide

🐦 @indycoffeeguide
📷 indycoffeeguide

WELCOME

We're thrilled to bring you the first ever *Scottish Independent Coffee Guide*. We've been combing the highlands and lowlands for the most exciting speciality roasters and coffee shops, where there's a whole bunch of lovely folk with huge passion for the mighty bean.

Across Scotland, artisan roasters are sourcing top quality green beans and carefully roasting them to bring out their natural flavour profiles.

Elsewhere, super skilled baristas are using these beans to create carefully crafted brews that pay respect to the long chain of people involved in the bean's journey – from the coffee farmer to the customer grabbing a flat white on the way to work.

'THERE'S A WHOLE BUNCH OF LOVELY FOLK WITH HUGE PASSION FOR THE MIGHTY BEAN'

There's loads of coffee in Scotland – some of it incredible, some not so good, but with your *Indy Coffee Guide* in your back pocket, you can be confident that you won't waste your precious and limited caffeine intake on anything but the very best speciality coffee. It's your starting point for some brilliant coffee adventures.

Enjoy!

Jo Rees
Editor

🐦 @indycoffeeguide
📷 indycoffeeguide

CONTENTS

THE ROAD TO PERFECTION

We commissioned eagle-eyed lensman Gavin Smart, to take a caffeine-fuelled journey to capture some of the characters behind Scotland's buzzing coffee scene

Leith Docks,
Edinburgh

James Aitken, roaster at
Dear Green Coffee Roasters
in Glasgow

Robi Lambie of
Cairngorm Coffee,
Edinburgh

Todd Whiteford and Katelyn Thomson of Avenue Coffee Roasting Co. in Glasgow

Gary Stone of Cult Espresso, Edinburgh

Jamie Craig of Filament Coffee, Edinburgh

Scott McGarry of Laboratorio
Espresso, Glasgow

Ellenabeich,
Argyll

Kilmore, Argyll

Mike Haggerton of Habitat Cafe, Aberfeldy

Road tripping in bonny Scotland

Simon Brown of Falcon Speciality Coffee, cupping at Steampunk Coffee

Edinburgh by
twilight

Scott Nicolson
of Steampunk
Coffee, North
Berwick

Danny Gorton of
Spitfire Espresso, Glasgow

Lisa Lawson of
Dear Green Coffee
Roasters in
Glasgow

Govan,
Glasgow

GAVIN SMART

'With many friends and my partner working in the speciality coffee world, this project for the Indy Coffee Guide really grabbed me,' says Edinburgh based photographer, Gavin. *'I wanted to capture the blood, sweat and tears that go into making this magical drink. So I took to the road to visit as many coffee folk as I could, to help share their stories and provide a glimpse under the hood of this exciting scene.'* See more of Gavin's photographs throughout the guide.

www.viewfromtheoutside.net

DEEP
IN THE CONGO

Death threats, land stolen by militia groups, mob rule and impassable roads. Schluter's Virunga Coffee project has got its work cut out, but is all the effort worth the reward?

The Schluter family set up its first office in what was then called the Belgian Congo in 1932. Since then Schluter has worked with many co-operative groups and local exporters, as well as having its own export companies.

Today the business is run by Phil Schluter, who's seen many changes in what is now the Democratic Republic of Congo (DRC). Phil says, *'we have been through so many ups and downs in the country, from the days of large volumes of exports in the 1950s and 1960s, through volcanic eruptions and the aftermath* of the Rwandan genocide in Goma, to the current collapse of robusta exports and the region's constant instability.

'There have been some great coffees – and some rather ropey ones – and years of great prices as well as terrible ones. There was even a time when we were flying green coffee from Goma down to Mombasa by plane because the high prices allowed for it.

'As a country, DRC has, in many ways, gone backwards over the last 50 years. In a country blessed with so many natural resources, it's a place of contrast between great natural wealth and extreme poverty. Much of the population is undernourished, yet anything you plant grows fast in the fertile soils with abundant rain and sunshine. However, militia groups often steal whatever is visible to feed themselves, so most of the population survive on root crops which lack key nutrients.'

'WE SEE JOY AND LAUGHTER ALL THE TIME, AND THERE'S HOPE THAT TOMORROW WILL BE BETTER THAN TODAY'

OPERATION VIRUNGA

The new Schluter company venture in DRC is called Virunga Coffee, with offices in Goma and Butembo in the Kivu region. They have constructed five wet mills, trained over 4,000 farmers and are proud to know them by name, with 1,800 of the farmers now benefiting from the higher premiums obtained through organic certification. Virunga has also set up five nurseries producing over 100,000 new seedlings per year and employs nine full time agronomists to train farmers.

These farmers are so important to Schluter that the company has looked to technology to give them a helping hand. *'We have all the organic farmers mapped on GPS and can see their farms using Google Maps. We also have photos of each, along with details of the farms and families.'*

This approach gives Schluter a level of traceability which helps it produce the finest

'RIGHT NOW WE HAVE CONTAINERS OF COFFEE WHICH HAVE BEEN BLOCKED ON THE SAME 50KM STRETCH FOR OVER THREE WEEKS'

coffee in optimum conditions, and offers a level of transparency which matches the best anywhere in the industry.

'We are now producing award winning fully-washed and organic coffees, and providing employment for hundreds of people,' says Phil. *'We provide our picking staff with food every day along with a salary which is higher than the local norm. We are also increasing the incomes of the thousands of smallholder farmers we work with.'*

DEATH THREATS

The project has had some pretty crazy challenges to deal with, as Phil explains, 'we have had two plots of land taken off us by militia groups, have received death threats when rival co-ops fell out, and have never-ending daily challenges operating in a country where the rule of law is seemingly almost entirely subjective!'

Everyday logistics are also a huge challenge. Coffee from Butembo is exported north via Beni, and then east through Uganda. The road from Butembo to Beni is 50km, and can be driven in under two hours on a good day. 'Unfortunately,' says Phil, 'at the moment there aren't many good days. Right now we have containers of coffee which have been blocked on the same 50km stretch for over three weeks.'

It is at times tempting to become cynical given all the challenges, but Schluter is 100 per cent committed to its vision for DRC. 'This is no short term sticking plaster, we are in it for the long haul and see it as the frontline of our company vision statement: "To transform lives in Africa through commerce in a mutually profitable way".'

Schluter is encouraged daily to see that things in Kivu are changing for the better, and – despite the many challenges – there is real progress in improving lives through improving coffee. 'It's so rewarding, we see joy and laughter all the time, and there's now hope that tomorrow will be better than today,' beams Phil.

In 2014 Virunga Coffee won 1st prize for the best DRC Coffee at the international AFCA coffee competition.

To find out more about the Schluter Virunga Project go to:
WWW.SCHLUTERCOFFEE.CO.UK

LESS
BUMP
IN THE GRIND?

Everything's going wireless these days. You can
be sipping a flat white in a cafe while tweaking the
temperature of the towel rail at home.
And as wireless technology hits the coffee world,
Cimbali's warning us to get ready for a
game changer

LET'S GET TECH

Technology is now enabling wireless connectivity between espresso
machines and grinders. One such example is Cimbali's PGS (Perfect
Grind System), which verifies the correct extraction and automatically
performs any corrections to the grind and dose.

THE SCIENCE

Why's that important? Best to start with the stats: to make a lip
smacking espresso, the rule (roughly) is that a perfect grind gives 25g
of coffee (plus or minus 2.5g), and takes 25 seconds (plus or minus 2.5)
to extract. If it's any different, the grind is not set correctly, and a bad
grind can wreck even the finest coffee. Too coarse and you get a light
coloured, weak, bitter espresso, too fine and it'll taste burnt and acrid.

'A BAD GRIND CAN WRECK EVEN
THE FINEST COFFEE'

CALLING ALL MILK-LOVERS

Wherever you buy our milk, rest assured we always pay our farmers a fair price for it. We've worked with some of them for over 20 years and, as farmers ourselves, we know everyone needs to make a living.

OUR MILK WILL ALWAYS:

✓ Come from our farm or The Organic Milk Suppliers Cooperative

✓ Come from cows fed on a pesticide and GM-free diet

✓ Come exclusively from British farms

✓ Taste great, the right way

FIND OUT MORE AT:
YEOVALLEY.CO.UK/MILKLOVERS

Yeo valley
FAMILY FARM

RETRO STYLE

Until now, to achieve this perfect grind ratio, the barista has had to tweak and fiddle with the grind to get it just right. This can vary for all sorts of maddening reasons such as room temperature and the weather, the skill of the barista and if the grinder woke up in a bad mood. But the biggest glitch with this – as well as the odd dodgy espresso – is the barista being so focused on the grinder that it takes him or her away from the opportunity to talk to customers.

THE PERFECT GRIND

Enter Cimbali's Magnum On Demand grinder-doser which is equipped with the PGS through bluetooth. The grinder-doser is in constant communication with the M34, M39 and M100 coffee machines with the PGS keeping a beady eye on the correct extraction of the espresso, and automatically performing any corrections to the grind. The result is maximum quality espresso – with minimal fiddling.

IS THIS THE FUTURE?

There are some compelling arguments for this new tech, including incredibly precise calibration (within 0.005mm) within the grinder, no cables (which are difficult to clean) and of course, an optimum cup of coffee.

All we need now is drone delivery of espresso through our bedroom window to coincide with the morning alarm going off. That's just months off, surely?

FULL OF
BEANS

Based at his professional training centre in
Edinburgh, John Thompson of Coffee Nexus is a
one man hotline to the coffee producing world

1

Explaining John Thompson's experience in the coffee world is a formidable task, but includes (for starters) his role as head judge at the international Cup of Excellence, an award scheme run across ten countries which helps farmers access high quality roasters.

Then there's his work with Speciality Coffee Association of Europe (SCAE) where he's helped develop its Coffee Diploma System and written content for

As a father of young children, John limits the number of trips he takes each year to four or five, but it's still his experience of working across the globe that sets him apart. At the end of last year, John even wrote a manual for the coffee board of Malawi (funded by the Scottish government which supports Malawi due to the Livingstone connection) to help small and medium farmers access highest value market share.

'COFFEE HAS NEVER TASTED AS GOOD AS IT DOES NOW'

the green coffee and sensory modules, *'to help improve the professional skill base of the speciality coffee community,'* says John.

And don't even get started on his work with numerous roasters and coffee brands – large and small. That can mean giving them certified pro training at his Edinburgh lab or going out to help improve and develop their roasting and procurement.

But his fave bit has to be travelling the coffee growing world, *'to work with farmers and improve sustainability in production, quality, and to help them diversify their product range,'* he says.

A passion for quality, diversity of coffee and the people behind the bean are key drivers, and John says, *'coffee links people across the world. It's great to have long term relationships and visit over the years. For me, it's all about the community and the development of coffee.'*

So he's feeling confident about the future of speciality coffee? *'Coffee has never tasted as good as it does now. It's a dynamic and evolving industry.'*

HOW DO THE EXPERTS DRINK COFFEE?

'I usually brew filter at home, and tend to reach for a Chemex or Kalita Wave most of the time.' says John. *'Once at work, I cup in the morning while my palate is fresh. The afternoon is more for product development or espresso tastings.*

'One thing I'm really keen on is having fresh coffee at home. If you get used to cupping coffee that's only a day old from the roaster, the change in the sensory profile as it starts to get stale is quite noticeable, so the coffee at home is always 10 days old or less.'

Coffee Nexus
8 Howard Street,
Edinburgh,
Midlothian, EH3 5JP.
www.coffeenexus.co.uk
01315 561430
f Coffee Nexus Ltd
🐦 @coffeenexus

NEW LIQUID ON THE BLOCK

Cascara is a drink that's making waves across the Scottish coffee scene. We got the lowdown from barista James Wallace

It might not sound like a gourmet liquid delight, but cascara (which means 'peel' in Spanish), is the husk from the dried skins of coffee cherries, a by-product of the coffee making process.

James Wallace is flying the cascara flag in Glasgow, saying, *'having cascara on your menu and offering samples makes people ask questions, and unlike coffee it's really flexible and easy to work with, so you can serve it almost*

'WHILE CASCARA ISN'T EXACTLY COFFEE, IT ISN'T TEA EITHER'

The pulped skins are collected after the coffee beans have been removed from the cherries and dried in the sun. The dried skins are then used to make a cool infusion that's hot in the coffee world right now.

As a natural product, cascara can be as diverse as the coffee beans themselves and packs a punch with sweet, fruity flavours and notes of cherry, redcurrant, mango or even tobacco. While cascara isn't exactly coffee, it isn't tea either, and curiosity about it is growing rapidly.

any way you can imagine. It also tastes great cold, far better than any iced coffee I've had.'

James plans to keep growing his cascara menu, *'I'd persuade everyone to give it a go, the more people who use it, the better the availability and quality will become.'*

If you can't decide whether you like coffee or tea best, now you can sort of have both – at once.

JAMES' SIGNATURE ORANGE AND BASIL CASCARA

Give it a go yourself with one of the recipes James was serving at the Glasgow Coffee Festival

1 Add 800g of boiling water to 48g of cascara and 5g of fresh basil leaves, preferably in a french press. Brew for 10 minutes.

2 Meanwhile take 300g of fresh orange juice and gently reduce by half in a pan.

3 Take a 11 litre Kilner jar and add 50g of honey through a funnel.

4 Once you've brewed and filtered the cascara mix, add this to the jar, then add the orange reduction.

5 Shake and spin the bottle to melt the honey into the mixture then place in an ice bath to rapidly chill. It will keep for around two weeks in the fridge.

6 To serve, add equal parts cascara syrup to tonic water, preferably over ice with a basil leaf for garnish.

JAMES WALLACE

Future of coffee?
'More crossover between baristas and mixologists'

Fave coffee shop?
'Silhouette in London'

James Wallace has been bitten hard by the coffee bug, saying: *'coffee was meant to just be a part-time job, but somewhere along the way it took over my life'*.
After competing in the 2014 UK Barista Championships, James had some tempting job offers but stayed in Glasgow. *'The coffee scene is moving so fast here, it's an exciting time, with room to really push the quality and consistency.'* This has led him to launch Back to Black, an event and pop-up speciality coffee brewer (see page 48).

★ GLASGOW COFFEE FESTIVAL

The 2015 festival was a barnstormer and perfectly reflected the caffeinated excitement that's brewing in the city

With over 35 exhibitors (a mix of local and international speciality coffee companies), cupping tasters, coffee talks with industry captains and even advice on how to wax your beard, the 2015 Glasgow Coffee Festival was buzzing with coffee folk from the moment the doors opened.

It was started in 2014 by Lisa Lawson of the city's Dear Green Coffee Roasters, who says, *'The Glasgow Coffee Festival was established in order to encourage an inspired coffee culture in a city where it hadn't quite hit yet, and thanks to our main sponsor La Marzocco, we were able to make it happen. I had nostalgic memories of Aroma Coffee Festival in Sydney, the Hawaii Kona Coffee Festival and MICE in Melbourne and try tearing me away from London Coffee Festival or a World of Coffee event! I felt that Scotland was seriously missing out!'*

UK ROASTING CHAMPS

The festival was also the site of the first ever SCAE (Speciality Coffee Association of Europe) UK Roasting Championship. *'It was great,'* says Lisa, *'as hosting an SCAE event added to the credibility and spectacle of the festival'.*

An intense and a fiercely fought competition, the UK's finest roasters went head to head over three days, making it quite a marathon.

Head judge Mans Akne Andersson says, *'The competition was set up to simulate the whole process of buying green coffee and looked at the knowledge required to assess coffee quality. We also looked at how the roasters created a plan for roasting and performed the roasting procedures to get an excellent cup. A group of judges then blind tasted and scored the coffee.*

'We were looking for execution, knowledge and a person who could present the best coffee. Coffee roasting is always a combination of knowledge about the coffee, sensory know-how and understanding of the technical aspects.'

AND THE WINNERS WERE?

Matthew Robley-Siemonsna of Prufrock took the top honours, while Alan Tomlins of Small Batch in Brighton came in second, and Edgars Juska of Vagabond and Prufrock was third (see right).

WWW.GLASGOWCOFFEEFESTIVAL.COM

Look out for an even bigger 2016 festival

GLASGOW
COFFEE
FESTIVAL

UK ROASTING
CHAMPIONSHIP
2015
sanctioned by SCAE UK
3rd

UK ROASTING
CHAMPIONSHIP
2015
sanctioned by SCAE UK
1st

UK ROASTING
CHAMPIONSHIP
2015
sanctioned by SCAE UK
2nd

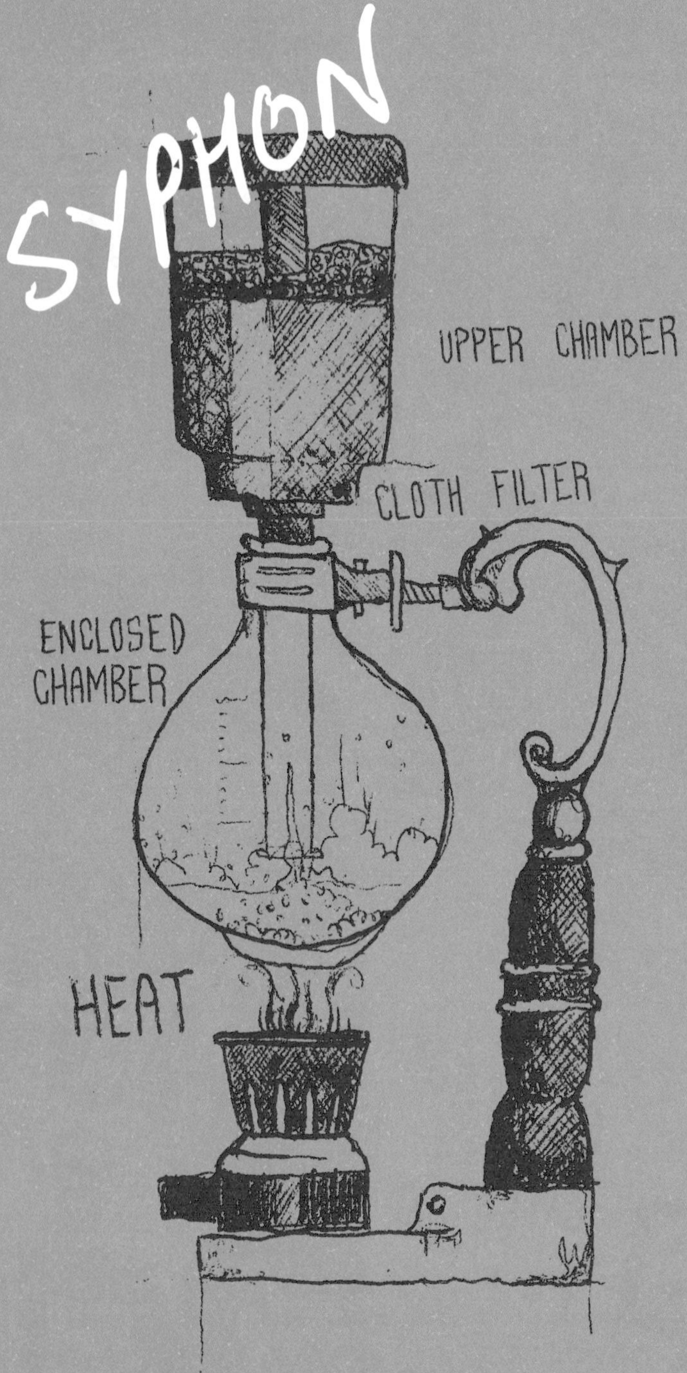

SYPHON

UPPER CHAMBER

CLOTH FILTER

ENCLOSED CHAMBER

HEAT

HOW TO USE THE GUIDE

VENUES

These are coffee houses, cafes and mobile coffee vans where you'll be able to drink a top notch cup.

ROASTERS

Meet the leading artisan coffee roasters in Scotland and discover where to source beans to use at home.

MORE GOOD CUPS AND ROASTERS

These are venues and roasters that also make the grade.

MAPS AND INDEX

We've split Scotland into areas to help you discover places that are near you, and every venue and roaster has a number, so you can find them either on the large map on the next page, or on the detailed area and city maps.

There's also an index at the back of the guide so you can search for businesses by name.

Don't forget to let us know how you get on as you explore Scotland's best speciality coffee venues and roasters:

🐦 @indycoffeeguide

📷 indycoffeeguide

SCOTLAND
by area

KEY

Coffee venues

Roasters

More good cups

More good roasters

Mobile coffee venues

All locations are approximate

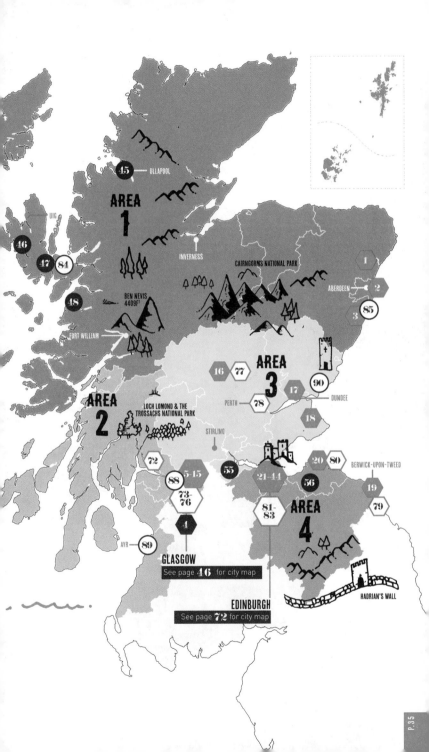

AREA 1

45 — ULLAPOOL

UIG

46

47 84

48

BEN NEVIS 4409FT

FORT WILLIAM

INVERNESS

CAIRNGORMS NATIONAL PARK

ABERDEEN — 2

1

3 85

AREA 2

LOCH LOMOND & THE TROSSACHS NATIONAL PARK

AREA 3

16 77

17

78

90

PERTH

DUNDEE

STIRLING

18

72

88

5-15

73-76

4

89

GLASGOW

21-44

55

20 80

56

BERWICK-UPON-TWEED

19

79

AREA 4

81-83

AYR

GLASGOW
See page 46 for city map

EDINBURGH
See page 72 for city map

HADRIAN'S WALL

VENUES

Impeccable places to drink coffee

AREA Nº 1

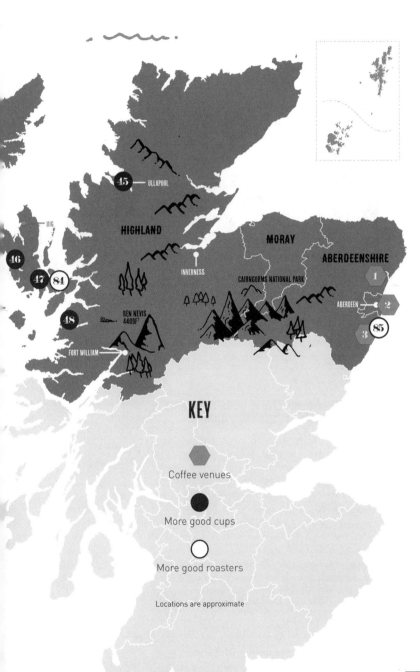

UIG

ULLAPOOL

HIGHLAND

MORAY

INVERNESS

ABERDEENSHIRE

CAIRNGORMS NATIONAL PARK

Aberdeen

BEN NEVIS
4409F¹

FORT WILLIAM

KEY

Coffee venues

More good cups

More good roasters

Locations are approximate

MAP Nº 1. THE COFFEE APOTHECARY

Udny, Ellon, Aberdeenshire, AB41 7PQ.

Travelling the world and experiencing different coffee cultures is a common starting point for countless coffee enthusiasts, and so it was for Jonny and Ali Aspden.

Three years travelling the globe and a couple of cups of particularly exceptional coffee was what it took to inspire them to bring speciality coffee to Aberdeenshire, and open The Coffee Apothecary.

INSIDER'S TIP THE EYE-CATCHING FLOOR IN THE BATHROOM GIVES A NEW MEANING TO "SPENDING A PENNY"

Taking over a *'tired village shop with potential'* and spending seven months stripping it back to the bare granite walls enabled them to create a cosy environment in which to sip speciality coffee, tuck in to home-cooked food and have a cheeky glass of wine or craft beer – under one roof.

In addition to offering Artisan Roast's Janszoon blend as espresso, they use what is possibly the first Marco SP9 machine in Scotland for making Chemex and V60, and there's a pleasing selection of loose leaf teas and luxury hot chocolate. You could spend the day here, starting with granola, fluffy pancakes and hearty cooked plates, and, when lunch kicks in, move on to baguettes and warming stews – all produced using local ingredients, as per Jonny and Ali's ethical ethos.

KEY ROASTER
Artisan Roast
Coffee Roasters

BREWING METHODS
Espresso, cafetiere, AeroPress, Chemex, V60

MACHINE
La Marzocco FB70

GRINDERS
Mahlkonig K30 Air, EK43

OPENING HOURS
Mon-Fri 7am-4pm
Sat 8am-4pm
Sun Closed

 Gluten FREE

 COFFEE BEANS AVAILABLE

 SOYA MILK AVAILABLE

 WIFI

 CYCLE FRIENDLY

 OUTDOOR seating

 FAMILY friendly

 DISABLED ACCESS

---

www.thecoffeeapothecary.co.uk   T: 01651 842253

f The Coffee Apothecary   🐦 @udnyapothecary   📷 thecoffeeapothecary

13-15 Thistle Street, Aberdeen, AB10 1XZ.

Us coffee geeks are pretty lucky really; usually, the venues serving cracking coffee are also creating some fantastic food – and it's no different at Foodstory in Aberdeen.

With a passion for wholesome grub and a drive to support the local community, the team at Foodstory strives to offer locally sourced, organic, homemade and vegan food at this neighbourhood cafe.

INSIDER'S TIP **CHECK OUT THE IMPRESSIVE CAKE STAND**

You'll find the same care going into the coffee, with owners Sandy and Lara designing a 4m long concrete coffee bar to house the La Marzocco Linea machine. A good range of pourover options sit alongside it, and there's a selection of Scottish and European roasters jostling for attention besides the Dear Green house blend.

Just like the coffee bar, most of the furniture at Foodstory has been handmade from recycled materials to create a happy and relaxed place to enjoy great food and coffee.

KEY ROASTER
Dear Green
Coffee Roasters

BREWING METHODS
Espresso, V60,
Chemex

MACHINE
La Marzocco
Linea

GRINDERS
Mazzer, Mahlkonig

OPENING HOURS
Mon 8am-5pm
Tue-Thu 8am-9pm
Fri 8am-10pm
Sat 9am-10pm
Sun Closed

www.foodstorycafe.co.uk

f Foodstory 🐦 @foodstorycoffee 📷 foodstoryaberdeen

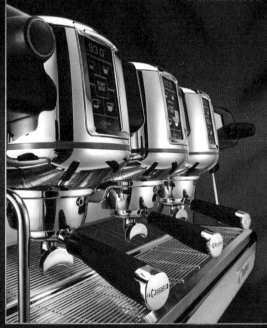

№3. BIG MOON COFFEE HOUSE

1 Bay View Apartments, Beachgate Lane, Stonehaven, AB39 2BD.

Lucia and Sean at Big Moon are expanding the horizons of the good coffee drinkers of Stonehaven. Not only through the tropical theme that pops up all over the cafe, but through their mission *'to convert people into coffee geeks'* as Lucia puts it.

Running a coffee shop wasn't what the pair planned on doing at all, but taking over the cafe from Lucia's parents a couple of years ago was the start of their personal journey through the world of coffee. As a whisky salesman previously, Sean had a developed palate, and by working with Todd at Avenue G and Lisa at Dear Green it's got better and better.

INSIDER'S TIP A REFURB, SYPHON AND DRIP TOWER ARE ON THE HORIZON - WATCH THIS SPACE

Now people have got wind that this is a place to find speciality coffee, Big Moon is developing a reputation and a good following, *'although it's still mainly with people who have lived away,'* says Lucia.

She's used the experience to develop her vegan baking, much of which is also gluten free (though you'd never tell) and so together, they've turned this seaside cafe into a must-visit.

KEY ROASTER
Avenue Coffee
Roasting Co.

BREWING METHODS
Espresso, Chemex

MACHINE
La Marzocco
Linea Classic
Custom

GRINDERS
Mazzer Super Jolly,
Mahlkonig K30 Vario

OPENING HOURS
Wed-Sun
10am-4.30pm

T: 01569 766991

 f Big Moon Coffee House 🐦 @bigmooncoffee 📷 bigmooncoffeehouse

AREA №2

ARGYLL AND BUTE

INVERARAY

LOCH LOMOND & THE
TROSSACHS NATIONAL PARK

DUMBARTON

WEST DUNBARTONSHIRE

EAST
DUNBARTONSHIRE

72

INVERCLYDE

4

49-51

86-87

5-15

88

73-76

RENFREWSHIRE

EAST
RENFREWSHIRE

NORTH AYRSHIRE

GLASGOW

See page 46 for city map

LAMLASH

89 — AYR

KEY

Coffee venues

Roasters

More good cups

More good roasters

SOUTH
AYRSHIRE

Mobile coffee venues

All locations are approximate

GLASGOW
City centre

KEY

Coffee venues

Roasters

More good cups

More good roasters

Mobile coffee venues

Roads

Rivers

· · · · · · · · · · · · · · · · · · · ·
Underground

· · · · · · · · · · · · · · · · · · · ·
Railway

All locations are approximate

№4. BACK TO BLACK

Mobile pop-up, Glasgow.

Back to Black may not have a permanent location, but that doesn't stop its team of top-notch baristas serving some extremely good coffee to the people of Glasgow.

Inspired by the coffee big guns – you know, Colonna & Smalls, 3FE, Prufrock and the like – owner James Wallace wanted to bring the same level of caffeine geekery to Scotland's second city. *'Our hope is to allow our guests to explore the incredible diversity of coffee,'* explains James. *'We opt for a science over craft approach, tracking down every variable and controlling them as best we can to improve consistency.'*

INSIDER'S TIP
JAMES HAS A OPEN-ALL-WEEK POP UP SHOP IN THE PIPELINE FOR EARLY 2016

Operating through a series of pop up brew bars and stalls in various locations around the city, these nomadic coffee hangouts not only offer signature brews but also expert advice for the budding home barista. Taking up a residency at Bakery 47 has had its benefits too, you'll find some kick-ass cakes and bakes accompanying the coffee – just the thought of the thyme and gruyère croissants have us drooling.

KEY ROASTERS
Five Elephant, Has Bean and guests

BREWING METHODS
EKspresso, batch brew, Kalita Wave

MACHINE
La Marzocco GS/3 AV

GRINDER
Modified EK43

OPENING HOURS
Varies by location - check social media

Gluten FREE

COFFEE BEANS AVAILABLE

SOYA MILK AVAILABLE

DISABLED ACCESS

www.backtoblackcoffee.co.uk   T: 07729437660

f Back To Black Coffee   🐦 @bcktoblckcoffee   📷 bcktoblckcoffee

MAP. Nº 5. GRACE & FAVOUR

11 Roman Road, Bearsden, Glasgow, G61 2SR.

There's certainly grace in the way that food and service are presented at this Bearsden Cross cafe, and its owner Susan has definitely done the community a favour in bringing speciality coffee to the neighbourhood.

However, for the true meaning of the Grace and Favour moniker, you need to look to the stag antlers adorning the walls. They were gifted to Susan by a lady who worked on the Balmoral Estate and lives in one of its grace and favour cottages, 'and now a tradition has started,' says Susan, 'as other people have started bringing them in too.'

INSIDER'S TIP 100 YARDS AWAY FROM A ROMAN BATH HOUSE, BUILT IN 142 AD

Just like the lofty origins of the decorations, Susan's set the bar high when it comes to food and drink. She's got local roaster, Home Ground, creating her house blend, installed an extensive range of teas from Edinburgh's PekoeTea, and has two bakers and two chefs working in-house, using nearly exclusively Scottish ingredients to create the cakes, pastries, scones and lunchtime dishes. The free range eggs are especially good (sourced from an Ayrshire farm), and in such demand that there's an "all day egg policy". Plump for the eggs benedict with Stornoway black pudding - it's cracking.

KEY ROASTER
Grace & Favour

BREWING METHODS
Espresso,
AeroPress

MACHINE
La Marzocco

GRINDERS
Mazzer Jolly,
Fiorenzato

OPENING HOURS
Mon-Sat
8.30am-5.30pm
Sun 9am-5pm

 Gluten FREE

 COFFEE BEANS AVAILABLE

 SOYA MILK AVAILABLE

 WIFI

 CYCLE FRIENDLY

 OUTDOOR SEATING

 FAMILY FRIENDLY

www.graceandfavourcoffee.com   T: 0141 5706501

f Grace & Favour   graceandfavourcoffee

MAP No 6. MEADOW ROAD

579 Dumbarton Road, Glasgow, G11 6RH.

One of the most distinctive features about this charming neighbourhood cafe and coffee shop is the handcrafted (and charmingly wonky) cups in which coffee is served.

They exemplify the Meadow Road approach to both coffee and food, which is all about the handmade and the carefully crafted. So peruse the long bar for its delightful array of homemade pastries, cakes, tarts and sarnies (vegan and veggies well represented), before grabbing a stool at the window to luxuriate in a brew with a bit on the side.

INSIDER'S TIP IN THE FAR REACHES OF THE WEST END, MEADOW ROAD IS A PERFECT SUNDAY BRUNCH DESTINATION

While espresso is made with Dear Green beans, AeroPress and V60 filters use the week's guest beans. And the best coffee/food combination? *'It has to be Colombian/Rwandan blend, served as a flat white with the house poached eggs with hot smoked salmon, avocado and spinach,'* says owner Kevan. We'll raise (a wonky) cup to that.

KEY ROASTER
Dear Green
Coffee Roasters

BREWING METHODS
Espresso, V60,
AeroPress

MACHINE
La Marzocco
Linea

GRINDER
Mazzer

OPENING HOURS
Mon-Fri 8am-5pm
Sat-Sun 9am-5pm

Gluten FREE

COFFEE BEANS AVAILABLE

SOYA MILK AVAILABLE

WiFi

CYCLE FRIENDLY

OUTDOOR SEATING

DISABLED ACCESS

DOG FRIENDLY

f Meadow Road 🐦 @meadowrdcoffee 📷 meadowroadcoffee

MAP No 7. KEMBER & JONES

134 Byres Road, Glasgow, G12 8TD.

The place to be spotted brunchin' in the city's West End since '04, there are few places that do coffee cool as well as Kember & Jones.

An institution on bohemian Byres Road, we challenge you to find a time when this independently owned café, deli and bakery isn't packed out with diners chowing down on artisan sandwiches, homemade cakes and evening specials. But it's worth the wait, if not for the vanilla poached pears with greek yoghurt, granola and honey, then for the handmade macarons.

INSIDER'S TIP DON'T MISS OUT ON KEMBER & JONES' SIGNATURE ROAST – GRAB A COFFEE TO GO IF THE TABLES ARE PACKED WITH PUNTERS

In 2010, owner Phil Kember decided to up the coffee game to match the cafe's made-from-scratch food philosophy, and now you'll find Kember & Jones' own small batch roasts in the grinders. With a Brazilian base, the signature house blend carries rich chocolate, caramel and toffee sweetness which craves a milky accompaniment – proper flat white material.

KEY ROASTER
Kember & Jones

BREWING METHODS
Espresso, filter

MACHINE
La Marzocco Linea

GRINDER
Mahlkonig K30 ground on demand

OPENING HOURS
Mon-Fri 8am-10pm
Sat 9am-10pm
Sun 9am-6pm

 Gluten FREE

 COFFEE BEANS AVAILABLE

 SOYA MILK AVAILABLE

 WIFI

 OUTDOOR seating

 FAMILY friendly

 DISABLED ACCESS

www.kemberandjones.co.uk   T: 0141 3373851

f Kember & Jones   🐦 @kemberandjones   📷 kemberandjones

COFFE

MAP No 8. AVENUE COFFEE

291 Byres Road, Glasgow, G12 8TL.

Positioned in the heart of Glasgow's bustling West End, Avenue Coffee has been expertly caffeinating Glasgow's coffee enthusiasts since opening its doors in 2011.

However, just serving a top quality cup wasn't enough for the owners, so shortly after opening a second shop in the city on Great Western Road, Avenue Coffee Roasting Co. came into being – on a Diedrich IR12 roaster.

Naturally, Avenue's own beans take centre stage on the espresso menu here, while guest roasts are available in three different filters on the AeroPress. Alongside the coffee offering there's also a delicious range of signature dishes from the cafe's kitchen with a solid lunch menu of soups, salads and sandwiches - be sure to try the house special eggs en cocotte (baked eggs) for breakfast.

INSIDER'S TIP ARRIVE EARLY ON THE WEEKEND FOR A PRIME PEOPLE WATCHING POSITION IN THE WINDOW

A popular spot with Glasgow's workforce and student population, it can get pretty busy at this little cafe come rush hour, but make a visit mid-afternoon and there are usually a few spots to cosy up in upstairs.

KEY ROASTER
Avenue Coffee
Roasting Co.

BREWING METHODS
Espresso,
AeroPress

MACHINE
La Marzocco
Linea

GRINDER
Mahlkonig K30

OPENING HOURS
Mon-Sun
8.30am-7pm

 Gluten FREE

 COFFEE BEANS AVAILABLE

 SOYA MILK AVAILABLE

 WIFI

 CYCLE FRIENDLY

 OUTDOOR seating

 FAMILY friendly

 COFFEE COURSES AVAILABLE

 DISABLED ACCESS

 DOG FRIENDLY

www.avenue.coffee   T: 0141 3395336

f Avenue Coffee   🐦 @avenue_coffee   📷 avenuecoffeeglasgow

MAP N° 9. ARTISAN ROAST GIBSON

15-17 Gibson Street, Glasgow, G12 8NU.

The Glaswegian contingent of the Artisan Roast clan, the Gibson Street venue has been keeping the city's West End well wired since setting up shop in 2009.

Taking tri-weekly deliveries of single origin beans from its roastery in Edinburgh, before grinding to order, you know the coffee here is going to be impeccably fresh and full of flavour. And leaving the roasting to its Eastern brothers means that the team at Gibson Street has the time to indulge in the coffee shop's second passion – food.

INSIDER'S TIP CHECK OUT THE LOCAL ARTISTS SHOWING OFF THEIR TALENTS IN THE GALLERY

A big chalk board behind the bar displays the day's foodie offerings – a small but intriguing collection of Instagram-worthy local, organic and vegan dishes. You'll want to save some of your daily food-gloating for the cakes though. They're far from the usual selection of bland bakes - visitors can look forward to snappin' delicious rose and pistachio shortbread and sinking their teeth into burstingly fruity blueberry danish pastries.

KEY ROASTER
Artisan Roast Coffee Roasters

BREWING METHODS
Espresso, V60, AeroPress, Chemex, cold brew, cafetiere

MACHINE
La Marzocco FB80

GRINDERS
Mahlkonig K30, Mazzer Major Electronic

OPENING HOURS
Mon-Thu 8am-8pm
Fri 8am-6.30pm
Sat-Sun 9am-6.30pm

 Gluten FREE

 COFFEE BEANS AVAILABLE

 SOYA MILK AVAILABLE

 WIFI

 CYCLE FRIENDLY

 OUTDOOR SEATING

 FAMILY FRIENDLY

 COFFEE COURSES AVAILABLE

 DISABLED ACCESS

 DOG FRIENDLY

www.artisanroast.co.uk   T: 07460854845

f Artisan Roast Glasgow   @artisanroastgla   artisan_roast_glasgow

MAP № 10. AVENUE COFFEE
321 Great Western Road, Glasgow, G4 9HR.

The younger, hipper brother of the West End venue, Avenue Coffee on Great Western Road is a brilliant find for the keen coffee connoisseur.

With an extensive brew bar which features (count 'em!) no less than seven brewing methods, three grinders and a team of highly skilled baristas, visitors to this working roastery are in for a unique experience with every cup.

After witnessing the baristas work their magic, sit back and get an insight into just how beans are turned from a raw green product into toasty, flavoursome little nuggets as you watch the roasters crafting, profiling and analysing from behind the glass on the mezzanine. It's the perfect way to appreciate the craft that goes into the drink you're imbibing. And if all that hard work (theirs, not yours), leaves you feeling peckish, there's a pile of croissants, cheese scones and bakes on the counter to get stuck in to.

INSIDER'S TIP
SEVEN DIFFERENT BREW METHODS MEANS SOMETHING DIFFERENT EVERY DAY OF THE WEEK

For those looking to broaden their barista skills, Avenue holds regular evening tasting sessions and brew classes too – keep an eye on its social media pages for dates.

KEY ROASTER
Avenue Coffee Roasting Co.

BREWING METHODS
Espresso, V60, AeroPress, Chemex, french press, Kalita, Clever dripper

MACHINE
La Marzocco Strada

GRINDERS
Mahlkonig K30, Ditting, Mythos One

OPENING HOURS
Mon-Fri
8.30am-5pm
Sat-Sun
9.30am-5pm

Gluten FREE

COFFEE BEANS AVAILABLE

SOYA MILK AVAILABLE

WIFI

CYCLE FRIENDLY

OUTDOOR SEATING

FAMILY FRIENDLY

COFFEE COURSES AVAILABLE

DISABLED ACCESS

DOG FRIENDLY

---

www.avenue.coffee   T: 0141 3391334

f Avenue Coffee   🐦 @avenue_coffee   📷 avenuecoffeeglasgow

Photos: Gavin Smart Photography www.viewfromtheroad.co.uk

11. LABORATORIO ESPRESSO

MAP:

93 West Nile Street, Glasgow, G1 2SH.

Photos: John Wood Photowork

A contemporary distillation of the Italians' idea of the good things in life: coffee, food and design, Laboratorio Espresso is a successful experiment in Glasgow.

An award winning interior provides a stunning backdrop to coffee that is seriously scientific, with every shot weighed and timed. You won't need to don a white coat to feel at home though, as owner Scot and team have harnessed a feel-good vibe in this modern interpretation of a traditional Milanese espresso bar.

INSIDER'S TIP FANS OF MODERNIST DESIGN WILL DELIGHT IN TAKING COFFEE IN AWARD WINNING SURROUNDINGS

'Glasgow is cosmopolitan,' says Scot, *'so we wanted to create a coffee experience that wouldn't be out of place in London, Berlin or Milan, while still being distinctly "Glasgow" - that is, stylish and friendly.'*

The bespoke house espresso blend comes courtesy of Has Bean, and is kept company by guest espressos from across the world including Workshop, The Coffee Collective, Five Elephant, The Barn and Common Man Roasters. And don't miss the chance to devour stunning pastries sourced directly from Italy, along with sandwiches from local institution Eusebi's.

KEY ROASTER
Has Bean

BREWING METHODS
Espresso,
AeroPress,
cold brew

MACHINE
La Marzocco
Linea

GRINDERS
Nuova Simonelli
Mythos, Mazzer
Super Jolly,
EK43

OPENING HOURS
Mon-Fri
7.30am-5.30pm
Sat 9am-5.30pm
Sun 11am-5.30pm

www.laboratorioespresso.com T: 0141 3531111

f Laboratorio Espresso @labespr labespr

12. SPITFIRE ESPRESSO

127 Candleriggs, Merchant City, Glasgow, G1 1NP.

Photos: Gavin Smart Photography www.viewfromtheoutside.net

N ew kid on the Glasgow coffee block, Spitfire Espresso only opened its doors in March 2015, but don't be fooled by its relative infancy, as owner Danny's been grinding beans with the pros for years in coffee-central, New Zealand.

Wanting to create something unique for his Spitfire house espresso, he's been working closely with Avenue Coffee Roasting Co. to perfect Gunnerbean, which is a smooth blend with a nutty, chocolatey edge. Drink it as espresso and pick out the delicate flavours, or experience it with milk in flat white form, while you watch bustling cafe life go by from the rustic wooden bar stools.

INSIDER'S TIP MAKE SURE TO COME ARMED WITH A HEALTHY APPETITE, AS THERE'S NO CHANCE YOU'LL RESIST THE ALL DAY EGGS AND HOMEMADE CAKES

The interior is bright and lively - we're talking revealed brick walls, reclaimed wood and flashes of red and blue furnishings - which match the super friendly welcome from Danny and the team. Plus, there's always a quirky playlist bringing this neighbourhood coffee spot to life.

KEY ROASTER
Avenue Coffee Roasting Co.

BREWING METHOD
Espresso

MACHINE
La Marzocco FB70

GRINDERS
Mazzer Major, Mazzer Super Jolly

OPENING HOURS
Mon-Sat 8am-6pm
Sun 10am-3pm

www.spitfireespresso.com T: 07578250105

f Spitfire Espresso 🐦 @spitfireglasgow 📷 spitfireglasgow

13. McCUNE SMITH

No.

3-5 Duke Street, Glasgow, G4 0UL.

It's not every day you come across sandwiches named after famous Scottish Enlightenment figures, but that's just the way things, um, roll at McCune Smith.

Named after Dr James McCune Smith, a graduate of the city and the first black American to earn a medical degree, this Glasgow coffee shop is all about supporting the little-man, from exhibiting emerging creatives' work on the cafe walls, to the local and ethical produce that stocks the kitchen.

INSIDER'S TIP NOTHING TO SEE HERE ... IN 2014 McCUNE SMITH WAS GIVEN A ONCE-OVER BY THE SECRET SERVICE, BEFORE A VISIT BY THE US AMBASSADOR

The simple and uncluttered interior, flooded with light from the floor to ceiling windows, is a great space in which to unwind and enjoy good coffee. Along with the Dear Green Rwandan single origin on espresso, you'll find a changing selection of guest roasters available on AeroPress and Kalita Wave.

There's also freshly baked cakes and a kooky collection of deli style sandwiches made with artisan bread - we're all over the Frances Wright: Kentucky style ham, homemade sweetcorn relish and salad on multigrain bread.

KEY ROASTER
Dear Green
Coffee Roasters

BREWING METHODS
Espresso,
Moccamaster drip,
AeroPress,
Kalita Wave

MACHINE
Royal Synchro

GRINDERS
Mazzer Super
Jolly Electronic,
Mahlkonig Tanzania

OPENING HOURS
Mon-Fri 8am-4pm
Sat 9am-5pm
Sun Closed

 Gluten FREE

 COFFEE BEANS AVAILABLE

 SOYA MILK AVAILABLE

 WIFI

 CYCLE FRIENDLY

 OUTDOOR seating

 FAMILY FRIENDLY

DISABLED ACCESS

DOG FRIENDLY

www.mccunesmith.co.uk   T: 0141 5481114

f McCune Smith Cafe   🐦 @mccunesmithcafe   mccunesmithcafe

№14. ALL THAT IS COFFEE

South Block, 60 Osborne Street, Glasgow, G1 5QH.

Crafting the perfect coffee is just another form of inspiring creativity at the Wasps' South Block artists studios in Glasgow.

The award winning building (it boasts the Doolan architecture prize) is home to Turner and Mercury Prize nominees, as well as All That Is Coffee, a contemporary, lively espresso bar that keeps the creatives buzzing.

The bright, airy space is ideal for meeting, ruminating, taking in the art on the walls, and of course exploring the ever changing guest roasts from Dear Green (its Goosedubbs espresso is the house blend).

INSIDER'S TIP FOR AN UNUSUAL SWEET TREAT, CHECK OUT THE SPANISH TORTA DE SANTIAGO

And it's easy to join in the banter with Fiona and her barista team who are at the heart of a friendly community of local businesses including a hairdressers, yoga studio and record store.

In addition to supporting a local roaster, hot chocolate, cakes and sandwiches are procured from local independents, while the 12 loose leaf teas come courtesy of PekoeTea in Edinburgh.

KEY ROASTER
Dear Green
Coffee Roasters

BREWING METHOD
Espresso

MACHINE
La Marzocco
Linea MP

GRINDERS
Mazzer, Mahlkonig

OPENING HOURS
Mon-Fri 9am-5pm

Gluten FREE

COFFEE BEANS AVAILABLE

SOYA MILK AVAILABLE

 WIFI

 DOG FRIENDLY

T: 0141 2714777

f All That is Coffee   🐦 @allthatiscoffee

15. TAPA ORGANIC

721 Pollokshaws Road, Strathbungo, Glasgow, G41 2AA.

An established Southside institution, Tapa Organic is as famous for its freshly baked breads and lazy weekend brunches as it is for speciality coffee.

A perk of having its own bakery down the road in Dennistoun is its selection of fabulous bread and cakes, and every day you'll find regulars at the coffee house scoffing the day's organic rye and sourdough bakes as if they were going out of fashion.

Along with the carb fest, there's also a good selection of vegan dishes from the in-house chefs, or go full-circle and pair your brew with Tapa's much loved all-day big breakfast.

INSIDER'S TIP BAD THINGS HAVE BEEN KNOWN TO HAPPEN IF TAPA RUNS OUT OF ITS FAMOUS MATCHA GREEN TEA LATTES

They like to get hands on here, so the team roasts its own beans on a brand spanking new roaster – known as Robyn. And as a result, they're looking forward to expanding the seasonally changing selection of single origin beans. Experience the flavours with a drink-in espresso or french press coffee, or pick up a bag of beans to experiment with at home.

KEY ROASTER
Tapa Coffee

BREWING METHODS
Espresso,
french press

MACHINE
La Marzocco Linea

GRINDER
Fiorenzato F83 E

OPENING HOURS
Mon-Sat
8am-6.30pm
Sun 9am-6.30pm

www.tapacoffee.com   T: 0141 4239494

f Tapa Organic   ✔@tapaorganic   tapaorganic

AREA № 3

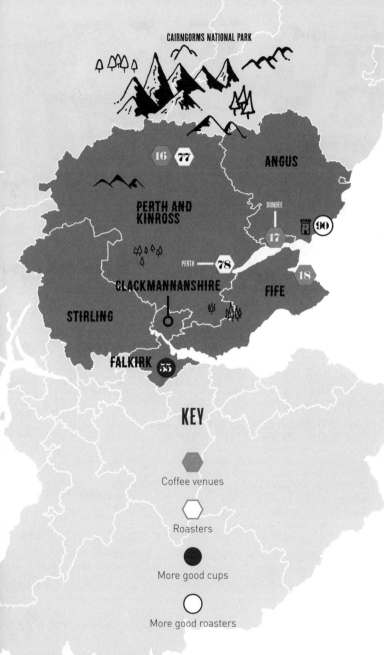

CAIRNGORMS NATIONAL PARK

ANGUS

16 77

PERTH AND
KINROSS

DUNDEE

17 90

PERTH 78

CLACKMANNANSHIRE

18

FIFE

STIRLING

FALKIRK 55

KEY

Coffee venues

Roasters

More good cups

More good roasters

All locations are approximate

MAP N° 16. HABITAT CAFE

1-2 The Square, Aberfeldy, Highland Perthshire, PH15 2DD.

This Antipodean-style coffee shop and cafe has become the heart of hip Aberfeldy since Mike and Jan Haggerton started it three years ago. Leaving a successful career in business consultancy to follow his coffee calling, Mike's channelled the drive, scientific thinking and attention to detail that he honed in his previous life to create the kind of coffee shop we all wish we had on our town square.

INSIDER'S TIP NOT EVERY AVAILABLE COFFEE AND BREW METHOD ARE ON THE MENU – ASK MIKE FOR AN OFF PISTE OPTION

You don't have to be a total coffee nut to make the trip to visit – its huge selection of 30 types of teas, and good cafe food (don't miss the burgers) are also a draw, but if you want to explore the world of the bean, then Mike's menu of 12 brew styles in total – from Chemex to syphon to AeroPress – as well as cracking espresso made with Has Bean beans, are a delight.

Touring? This cool little town with its retro cinema, good restaurants, funky boutiques, roastery (Glen Lyon), music festival and, of course, brilliant coffee shop, make Aberfeldy an absolute must-visit.

KEY ROASTER
Has Bean

BREWING METHODS
Espresso, V60, AeroPress, Chemex, Clever, Woodneck, Kalita Wave, syphon, Phin

MACHINE
3 Group Nuova Simonelli Aurelia II T3

GRINDERS
Compak K10, Mahlkonig Guatemala

OPENING HOURS
Seasonal

 Gluten FREE

 COFFEE BEANS AVAILABLE

 SOYA MILK AVAILABLE

 WIFI

 CYCLE FRIENDLY

 OUTDOOR seating

 FAMILY FRIENDLY

 DISABLED ACCESS

 DOG FRIENDLY

www.habitatcafe.co.uk T: 01887 822944

f Habitat Cafe 🐦 @habitatcafe 📷 habitatcafeaberfeldy

MAP Nº 17. PACAMARA FOOD AND DRINK

302 Perth Road, Dundee, DD2 1AU.

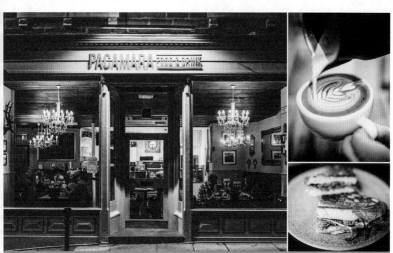

Dundee's speciality coffee cafe has been known and loved as Espress Oh! since 2013, with proprietor Barry Thomson introducing Has Bean beans expertly pulled though the La Spaziale - with AeroPress as an added option.

Now, in a new phase of the business, he's rebranded as Pacamara, after the famed bean, and is developing the food and other drinks to match the quality of the coffee.

INSIDER'S TIP
PACAMARA'S REUBEN SANDWICH HAS BEEN ON THE MENU FROM DAY ONE AND IS AN ABSOLUTE FAVE WITH REGULARS

'We changed the name because we wanted one that was synonymous with speciality coffee but didn't suggest we were only a coffee shop, because everything we are doing with food, wine and craft beer is just as important.'

Breakfast and lunch is served seven days a week, as well as brunch specials such as french toast with caramelised banana on the weekend. For dinner, think flat iron steak (cooked sous vide then finished off on the chargrill for both succulence and flavour) with handmade, triple cooked chips.

It can be difficult carrying off a daytime-into-evening look, but the homely feel that comes with the wooden tables and upcycled chairs, along with chandeliers, only needs a change of lighting to feel very bistro.

KEY ROASTER
Has Bean

BREWING METHODS
Espresso,
AeroPress

MACHINE
La Spaziale S9

GRINDERS
Mahlkonig K30,
Mahlkonig EK43

OPENING HOURS
Mon-Tue 9am-5pm
Wed-Fri
9am-5pm and
6pm-10pm
Sat 9.30-5pm
and 6pm-10pm
Sun 10am-4pm
and 6pm-10pm

 COFFEE BEANS AVAILABLE

 SOYA MILK AVAILABLE

 OUTDOOR seating

 FAMILY friendly

  DOG FRIENDLY

www.pacamara.co.uk   T: 01382 527666

f Pacamara Food & Drink   🐦 @pacamaradundee   📷 pacamaradundee

Ed Gooding • ed.gooding@bunn.com
Mobile: +44 (0) 778 751 0062 • **Office:** +44 (0) 121 745 8104

18. ZEST CAFE

95 South Street, St Andrews, Fife, KY16 9QW.

There's one aim for individuals working at Zest Cafe and that's to be the barista in charge of the Marzocco. *'And everyone wants to do the latte art – it's a real motivator,'* smiles cafe owner Lisa Cathro.

Training is taken seriously at Zest – three of the team trained in Holland to become Professional level SCAE trainers in Barista Skills. Part of Zest's raison d'être is to work with people who have additional needs and barriers to employment, something for which it's won many awards.

Two espresso choices are on offer, Red Stag from Glen Lyon for a light roast, which is full bodied and sweet, and Grumpy Mule's Widescreen blend, a medium roast with caramel, biscuit and malty flavours.

INSIDER'S TIP ZEST SUPPORTS THE STANZA POETRY FESTIVAL WITH AN OPEN MIC POETRY EVENT

Lisa first encountered speciality coffee while working in Australia, but says she really turned into a *'complete coffee geek'* when she began seriously training, a love she's spread to all members of the team.

The Zest story began about eight years ago, and it's grown organically to become a much loved port of call for breakfast and lunch – as well as great coffee, of course.

KEY ROASTER
Glen Lyon
Coffee Roasters

BREWING METHODS
Espresso, filter

MACHINE
La Marzocco

GRINDERS
Mahlkonig K30,
Ceado

OPENING HOURS
Mon-Sun 8am-6pm

 Gluten FREE

 SOYA MILK AVAILABLE

 WIFI

 CYCLE FRIENDLY

 OUTDOOR SEATING

 FAMILY FRIENDLY

 COFFEE COURSES AVAILABLE

DISABLED ACCESS

 DOG FRIENDLY

www.zest-standrews.com   T: 01334 471451

f Zest Cafe   🐦 @zeststandrews

NORTH BERWICK

20 **80**

EAST LOTHIAN

56

BERWICK-UPON-TWEED

81-83

57-71

21-44

19

WEST LOTHIAN

79

MIDLOTHIAN

EDINBURGH

See page **72** for city map

SCOTTISH BORDERS

HADRIAN'S WALL

KEY

Coffee venues

Roasters

More good cups

All locations are approximate

№19. RIALTO COFFEE CO.

33 High Street, Eyemouth, Berwickshire, TD14 5EY.

Just ten miles from the Scottish border, Rialto Coffee Co in Eyemouth should certainly be the first speciality coffee venue you visit at the start of your coffee tour of Scotland.

With the serene Berwickshire coast as its backdrop, this neighbourhood coffee shop is dedicated to serving its local community and tempting road trippers and caffeine tourists to the historic fishing town it calls home. And with a well-rounded cup of freshly ground, single origin beans from Avenue Coffee Roasting Co. as bait, they're biting.

INSIDER'S TIP HOP OFF THE A1 A LITTLE EARLY AND PARK UP RIGHT OUTSIDE THIS COFFEE HAUNT FOR THE ULTIMATE SPECIALITY PIT STOP

The Howes-Quintero family, who've run Rialto since 2014, is also luring visitors with a glorious selection of innovative soups, sandwiches and bakes, which certainly live up to the standard of the fantastic speciality coffee. The menu changes with the seasons, using fabulously fresh local produce when possible and everything is handmade everyday from scratch.

KEY ROASTER
Avenue Coffee Roasting Co.

BREWING METHOD
Espresso

MACHINE
La Marzocco Linea PB

GRINDER
SV Italia SAB

OPENING HOURS
Tue-Sat 9am-4pm
Changes with seasons, please check website

www.rialto-coffee.uk T: 01890 752048

f Rialto Coffee Co. RialtoCoffeeCo

20. STEAMPUNK COFFEE

49a Kirk Ports, North Berwick, East Lothian, EH39 4HL.

Sharing the same former industrial joinery as its roastery, Steampunk is not your usual coffee house.

Split over two levels, a funky old warehouse has been transformed into both a working artisan coffee roastery and a welcoming environment in which to showcase the (lip smacking) results.

INSIDER'S TIP CATCH STEAMPUNK'S VW COFFEE VAN AT EDINBURGH'S STOCKBRIDGE MARKET ON SUNDAYS

Downstairs, you'll find a cool copper bar supporting the resident Linea Classic machine, and visitors can sample the espresso offerings in the communal seating area. The roasters and baristas are always playing around with brew methods to get the best cup out of the beans, so don't hesitate to pick their brains. Upstairs there are comfy armchairs and a cosy log fire just waiting to be enjoyed with a flat white and slab of homemade cake (taking along your slippers is optional).

A big noise in the North Berwick scene, you'll find local produce in the savoury bites coming from the kitchen, and a cracking line-up of events promoting home-grown talent – keep an eye on its social media pages for dates.

KEY ROASTER
Steampunk Coffee

BREWING METHODS
Espresso,
Bunn batch brewer

MACHINE
Linea Classic

GRINDER
Mythos One

OPENING HOURS
Mon-Sat 9am-5pm
Sun 10am-5pm

 Gluten FREE

 COFFEE BEANS AVAILABLE

 SOYA MILK AVAILABLE

 WIFI

 CYCLE FRIENDLY

 OUTDOOR seating

DISABLED ACCESS

 DOG FRIENDLY

www.steampunkcoffee.co.uk T: 01620 893030

f Steampunk Coffee 🐦 @steampunkcoffee 📷 steampunkcoffee

EDINBURGH
City centre

KEY

Coffee venues

Roasters

More good cups

More good roasters

Roads

Rivers

Tram

Railway

MAP Nº **21.** ARTISAN ROAST STOCKBRIDGE

100a Raeburn Place, Edinburgh, EH4 1HH.

offee and flowers may not be as well known or as natural a pairing as coffee and cake, but Artisan Roast's latest venture is turning these strange bedfellows into "a thing".

Honouring its roots in Scottish speciality coffee, Artisan Roast Stockbridge is a go-to spot for sensational single-origins, extensive brewing options and a level of coffee-geekery that's, dare we say it, strangely sexy.

But the waft of freshly ground beans in the air also mingles with the heady scent of luscious roses and the sharp tang of foliage, as this branch of the Artisan Roast family is also somewhere to pick up a beautiful bunch of blooms from the in-house florist.

INSIDER'S TIP
GRAB A BAG OF FRESHLY ROASTED COFFEE TO TAKE HOME – YOU'LL FIND A GOOD SELECTION STOCKING THE SHELVES

And if that wasn't stimulation enough for the senses, you should also visit for the fab line-up of live music from local musicians, along with a lust-worthy lunch offering of rustic sandwiches, toasty soups and sumptuous cakes. It's euphoric sensual overload ...

KEY ROASTER
Artisan Roast Coffee Roasters

BREWING METHODS
Espresso, V60, AeroPress, Chemex

MACHINE
La Marzocco GB5

GRINDER
Mazzer Family

OPENING HOURS
Mon-Fri
8.30am-6pm
Sat-Sun 9am-5pm

---

www.artisanroast.co.uk   T: 07542314280

f Artisan Roast _ Stockbridge   🐦 @artisanroast   📷 artisan_roast

22. PEKOETEA

55 Raeburn Place, Edinburgh, EH4 1HX.

When a cafe which serves more than 100 loose teas and infusions from around the world decides to start serving coffee, the bar is set high.

'We decided that we had to provide the same high level of coffee as we do tea,' says Jon Cooper, the man behind PekoeTea, Edinburgh's speciality tea merchants. It's a promise from a perfectionist.

So the team buys beans weekly and sells them within a fortnight. *'There is nothing older than six weeks on our shelves, ever,'* reiterates Jon.

INSIDER'S TIP TRY A MATCHA TEA, MADE TO PERFECTION WITH A BAMBOO WHISK

Coffee comes from Glasgow-based roaster Dear Green, with Goosedubbs the main blend, and alternating single estates available on the V60. Every single shot is weighed and the machines are scrupulously clean.

High spec though this is, you won't find latte art, as the focus is on crafting the very best espresso and V60 – served by skilled baristas. *'Regular training is really important. We go for consistency, as the flavour has to be right every time.'*

Grab your coffee and an accompanying macaron or financier, and enjoy perusing the shelves of tea caddies, jostling alongside teaware and coffee brewing equipment.

KEY ROASTER
Dear Green
Coffee Roasters

BREWING METHODS
Espresso, V60

MACHINE
Racillio Class 7

GRINDER
Fiorenzato

OPENING HOURS
Mon closed for now
Tues-Sat 10am-6pm
Sun 11am-5pm

www.pekoetea.co.uk   T: 0131 6292420
f PekoeTea 🐦 @pekoetea 📷 pekoetea_edinburgh

MAP 23. LEO'S BEANERY

23a Howe Street, Edinburgh, EH3 6TF.

A uthentic family-run cafes are hard to come by these days, but we think we may have found the real deal at Leo's Beanery in the New Town.

Establishing the neighbourhood coffee spot six years ago, husband and wife, Joe and Marie have given the space a homely touch, hand crafting the furniture from old church pews and decorating the walls with black and white images of grandparents and great grandparents.

With such a personal feel, it was only right to create a signature house blend on the coffee front, so after working closely with roaster Hands-On, Leo's 80/20 was born. You'll also find a guest roast on the grinder, featuring the team's current fave. Recent residencies include Rounton Coffee's "blueberry bomb", Rocko Mountain.

INSIDER'S TIP LEO'S IS NAMED AFTER OWNER JOE'S GRANDFATHER

Lovingly home-cooked food is the order of the day, especially brekkie (for which it's famed), such as chewy local bagels or the real deal of local bacon and black pudding, wilted spinach and vine tomatoes, for example. At lunch, chow down on chunky sarnies, or the signature burger and award winning orange and almond cake.

KEY ROASTER
Hands-On

BREWING METHOD
Espresso

MACHINE
La Marzocco

GRINDER
Mazzer Super Jolly

OPENING HOURS
Mon-Fri 8am-5pm
Sat 9am-5pm
Sun 10am-5pm

Gluten FREE

COFFEE BEANS AVAILABLE

SOYA MILK AVAILABLE

WIFI

CYCLE FRIENDLY

OUTDOOR seating

FAMILY friendly

DOG FRIENDLY

www.leosbeanery.co.uk   T: 0131 5568403

f Leo's Beanery   🐦 @leosbeanery   📷 leosbeanery

24. TWELVE TRIANGLES

90 Brunswick Street, Edinburgh, EH7 5HU.

Hollie and Rachel, two friends with a love of baking and a sense of adventure, set up Edinburgh cake shop, Lovecrumbs, four years ago. Although initially a wholesale bakery business, within six months they'd started a shop, and soon, spurred on by a desire to create a sociable space around the bakery, Lovecrumbs began serving coffee alongside the cakes.

Then came little sister, Twelve Triangles, which opened last year just off the beaten track at Leith Walk. It's already cemented its place in the local community, serving Steampunk coffee and fixes for sugar cravings.

INSIDER'S TIP
CHECK OUT THE FABULOUS "GREEN WALL" MINI GARDEN

'Some customers pop in for a brew up to three times a day', say the pair, and it seems not many can resist the doughnuts with flavours such as passion fruit and homemade ricotta, or bramble jam. Everything produced by Hollie and Rachel is top quality, so you'll find tea from Anteaques, chocolate from Coco, cold brew from Brew Lab, and Kitsch and Roots soda. *'We've a simple aim,'* says Hollie, *'we want people to come and have the best coffee in the area.'*

KEY ROASTER
Steampunk Coffee

BREWING METHOD
Espresso

MACHINE
La Spaziale

GRINDER
Anfim

OPENING HOURS
Mon-Fri 8am-5pm
Sat 9am-5pm
Sun 10am-5pm

COFFEE BEANS AVAILABLE

SOYA MILK AVAILABLE

DOG FRIENDLY

---

www.twelvetriangles.co.uk   T: 0131 6294664

f TwelveTriangles   🐦 @twelvetriangles   📷 twelvetriangles

Drinks
Gear
Knowledge

The home of Sweetbird, Zuma and Cosy Tea has been supplying the coffee scene for over 18 years, and is a proud supporter of the Scottish Coffee Guide

0117 953 3522

OOO @beyondthebean

ARTISAN ROAST BROUGHTON

57 Broughton Street, Edinburgh, EH1 3RJ.

One of the original sparks to ignite the explosion of artisan coffee in Scotland, Artisan Roast was the first speciality coffee shop and roastery in the country. First opening its doors in 2007, the Broughton Street branch is where it all began, and even though the roastery has outgrown its home and made a new one nearby, the cafe remains one of the city's busiest coffee hangouts.

Along with an extensive range of brewing methods and a good selection of espressos pulled through the sleek Mirage Kees van der Westen machine, the coffee shop offers hot soups and a delicious range of bakes, as well as a superior class of banter and advice, plus lost key storage for those who pass through.

INSIDER'S TIP GRAB A SEAT IN THE BACK ROOM AND CHALLENGE A FELLOW COFFEE FIEND TO A GAME OF BATTLESHIPS

Racking up an impressive number of awards, its baristas are your go-to guys for the lowdown on the latest equipment and brewing at home. Plus, the open-plan layout of the cafe means there's (literally) no bar between customers and the caffeine professionals.

KEY ROASTER
Artisan Roast Coffee Roasters

BREWING METHODS
Espresso, V60, AeroPress, Chemex, cafetiere

MACHINE
Kees van der Western Mirage Idrocompresso

GRINDERS
Mahlkonig K30, Mazzer Major

OPENING HOURS
Mon-Thu
8am-7.30pm
Fri 8am-6.30pm
Sat-Sun
9am-6.30pm

www.artisanroast.co.uk   T: 07713511747

f Artisan Roast   🐦 @artisanroast   📷 artisan_roast

26. FORTITUDE COFFEE

3c York Place, Edinburgh, EH1 3EB.

Being one of Edinburgh's tiniest coffee shops, and surrounded by big name neighbours such as the National Portrait Gallery and The Stand Comedy Club, you could easily miss Fortitude Coffee on York Place – but you really shouldn't, as this is a caffeinated hotspot worth seeking out.

INSIDER'S TIP THE FLOORING HERE IS RECLAIMED FROM AN OLD CHURCH AND THE SHELVES MADE FROM IROKO STACKING CRATES

Not only does it sell a good range of beans, ground to order for customers' preferred brewing method at home, but its in-house offering is seriously impressive. Showcasing speciality roasters from around the UK and Europe, this is your chance to root out a new fave. There's always something novel to try with a weekly guest espresso as well as two options for pourover and AeroPress serve styles.

You'll be lucky to find a seat (we weren't kidding when we said it was small), as this is a popular spot, but if you can grab a pew in the window, make sure to watch the trams go by with slice of cake from local bakery, Lovecrumbs.

KEY ROASTER
Workshop Coffee

BREWING METHODS
Espresso, pourover, AeroPress

MACHINE
La Marzocco Linea PB

GRINDERS
Anfim Super Caimano, Mahlkonig Tanzania

OPENING HOURS
Mon–Fri 8am-6pm
Sat 10am-6pm
Sun 11am-4pm

www.fortitudecoffee.com   T: 0131 5573063

f Fortitude Coffee   @fortitudecoffee   fortitudecoffee

MAP № 27. URBAN ANGEL

121 Hanover Street, Edinburgh, EH2 1DJ.

It's not always easy to find somewhere where the food menu lives up to the coffee offering, but Urban Angel in Edinburgh is acing both.

With the philosophy that wholesome, organic and delicious food should be enjoyed every day, not just on special occasions [our kinda' thinking], you can expect a tempting array of breakfast, brunch and lunch dishes from the kitchen of this humble cafe. From the almond milk and peanut butter packed smoothies, to the jam and ricotta smothered freshly baked bread, most of the menu is made in-house, using local and seasonal Scottish produce.

INSIDER'S TIP
TRY MORE OF URBAN ANGEL'S DELISH FOOD AT EVENING DINING EVENTS THROUGHOUT THE YEAR

The coffee line-up certainly honours the chef's hard graft, with North Star, Alchemy and Caravan roasters all having regular stints in the grinders. There's a comprehensive range of brewing methods to match the top quality beans, too, with cold brew making an appearance in summer. Grab a seat outside when the sun's shining and bask in the complex flavours of the chilled coffee.

KEY ROASTERS
North Star Coffee Roasters, Alchemy

BREWING METHODS
Espresso, Bunn batch brew, AeroPress, cold brew

MACHINE
La Marzocco Linea 2 Group

GRINDERS
Nuova Simonelli Mythos One, Mahlkonig Tanzania

OPENING HOURS
Mon-Fri 8am-5pm
Sat-Sun 9am-5pm

Gluten FREE

COFFEE BEANS AVAILABLE

SOYA MILK AVAILABLE

WIFI

CYCLE FRIENDLY

OUTDOOR seating

FAMILY friendly

---

www.urban-angel.co.uk   T: 0131 2256215

f Urban Angel   🐦 @urbanangelcafe   📷 urbanangel_cafe

№28. WELLINGTON COFFEE

33a George Street, Edinburgh, EH2 2HN.

Take a break from the city centre shops and head to the corner of George and Hanover Street, then follow the railings and slip down the steps to the tiny pit stop that's Wellington Coffee.

Perfect for anyone craving the purity of experience that comes from enjoying perfectly made coffee, Wellington focuses on espresso from the Synesso machine and three Mythos grinders. Yes, there is a small selection of cakes, but this place is really only about one thing. Nice and simple.

The main roaster is Square Mile but bi-weekly guest coffees – sourced from Europe to Australia – provide plenty of choice and the chance to sample some of the newest roasts around.

INSIDER'S TIP ENJOY THE OUTSIDE SEATING AREA ON A SUNNY DAY

A feeling of sanctuary is reflected in the lack of "noise" about Wellington; there's not much online presence and no Wi-Fi, but once inside you'll find good old fashioned one-to-one hospitality from the knowledgeable and efficient staff.

KEY ROASTER
Square Mile
Coffee Roasters

BREWING METHOD
Espresso

MACHINE
Synesso

GRINDER
Mythos

OPENING HOURS
Mon-Fri 7am-6pm
Sat 8am-6pm
Sun 9am-6pm

COFFEE BEANS AVAILABLE

SOYA MILK AVAILABLE

CYCLE FRIENDLY

OUTDOOR SEATING

DOG FRIENDLY

T: 0131 2256854

MAP Nº 29. CAIRNGORM COFFEE

41a Frederick Street, Edinburgh, EH2 1EP.

H and crafted and roughly hewn are the best descriptions of Cairngorm Coffee, and apply to the stone wall bar as much as to the doorstep grilled cheese sarnies - which would keep a highland crofter going for a couple of days in bad weather.

Robi and team may be located in the middle of elegant Georgian Edinburgh, but their basement coffee shop speaks more of the rustic than of Palladian architecture.

A passion for authenticity also runs through the menu, which is peppered with artisan chilli jam, bagels, brownies, and of course cheese. Naturally, coffee for its Red Hills espresso is sourced from Mr Eion, just ten minutes away.

INSIDER'S TIP FIND AN ADDITIONAL GUEST ESPRESSO FROM THE LIKES OF EXTRACT AND SMALL BATCH

Expect to be served a top quality coffee from the experienced baristas, and while there is always a filter option (mainly V60 but sometimes AeroPress, pending on the best fit for the guest filter) available, *we are particularly obsessed with exploring different espresso recipes,'* explains Robi.

Track it down for a bracing blast of rejuvenation in the city.

KEY ROASTER
Mr Eion Coffee
Roaster

BREWING METHODS
Espresso, V60,
AeroPress

MACHINE
La Marzocco
Linea 2 Group

GRINDERS
Mahlkonig K30 Dual,
Mazzer Robur

OPENING HOURS
Mon-Fri
7.30am-7pm
Sat-Sun
9am-6pm

Gluten FREE

COFFEE BEANS AVAILABLE

SOYA MILK AVAILABLE

WIFI

OUTDOOR SEATING

DOG FRIENDLY

---

www.cairngormcoffee.com   T: 0131 6291420

f Cairngorm Coffee Co.   🐦 @cairngormcoffee   cairngormcoffeeco

30. CASTELLO COFFEE CO.

7a Castle Street, Edinburgh, EH2 3AH.

This tiny little coffee shop (more a kiosk really) in the heart of Edinburgh's shopping district, is a mecca for espresso lovers, and has been voted Best Coffee Shop in the city in two out of the three years it's been open, as well as number one of a hundred espressos in Edinburgh.

Hidden in plain sight, you have to be in the know to find it (which you are now, happily), but once you do, you'll almost certainly return for drop of liquid gold, care of its Allpress house espresso, as well as Nude, Dear Green and Climpson and Sons guest roasts.

INSIDER'S TIP DON'T LEAVE WITHOUT TRYING THE TOASTED COCONUT BREAD

On the food front, visit for homemade vegan and veggie soups, and freshly prepped focaccia sandwiches.

Sandro del Greco's friendly coffee shop has great views of the castle (the clue's in the name, of course), and what it lacks in space, it makes up for in outdoor seating, so in summer it's a bike and dog-friendly pit stop, as well as somewhere to recharge during a dose of retail therapy.

KEY ROASTER
Allpress Espresso

BREWING METHOD
Espresso

MACHINE
La Marzocco
GB/5

GRINDERS
Mythos One,
Mazzer Kony

OPENING HOURS
Mon–Fri
7.30am–6pm
Sat 8.30am–6pm
Sun 10am–6pm

T: 0131 2259780

f Castello Coffee Co.   @castellocoffee   castellocoffee

MAP.Nº 31. THE COUNTER

Police Box, Lothian Road, Usherhall, Edinburgh, EH1 2DJ.

Quite possibly one of the smallest coffee shops in Britain, let alone Scotland, The Counter is a former police box, rescued by husband and wife team Alastair and Sally McFarlane. The pair are not only passionate about restoring and renovating "at risk" buildings, happily, they also happen to be rather good at making coffee.

Alastair and Sally first fell in love with the mighty bean on their travels in San Francisco, although a shared background in hospitality had already nurtured a keen eye for quality and service. On their return home, they were looking for somewhere to set up a coffee shop when they spotted the broken and rather sad looking blue box on the corner of Lothian Road.

INSIDER'S TIP THE SALTED CARAMEL BROWNIES ARE A BITE-SIZED PIECE OF PERFECTION

The Counter opened in 2014 and, with 140 similar boxes around the city, it's no surprise Ali and Sally have converted another two – at Tollcross and Morningside. Visit to try the house blend of dark roasted Sumatran and Brazilian beans from Mr Eion, along with baked treats, homemade by Ali. Space is – of course - limited, so they keep to a select, but rotating menu of six items – all matched to the coffee.

KEY ROASTER
Mr Eion Coffee Roaster

BREWING METHOD
Espresso

MACHINE
SanRemo Zoe 2 Group Compact

GRINDER
SanRemo Stardust

OPENING HOURS
Mon-Fri
7.30am-3pm

COFFEE BEANS AVAILABLE

SOYA MILK AVAILABLE

CYCLE FRIENDLY

FAMILY FRIENDLY

DISABLED ACCESS

DOG FRIENDLY

f The Counter   🐦 @thecountered   📷 thecountered

№32. HULA JUICE BAR AND GALLERY

103-105 West Bow, Edinburgh, EH1 2JP.

A little taste of the tropics in the centre of Edinburgh, Hula Juice Bar and Gallery on West Bow isn't your usual artisan coffee spot.

With an enticing collection of exotic juice blends, fabulous fruit bowls and creative salads, all with names that will leave you craving an escape to sunny climes (think Sunshine in a Cup and Blue Hawaiian), and a colourful interior, this is the place to head for a reprieve from the Edinburgh winter.

INSIDER'S TIP BREAKFAST IS THE MOST IMPORTANT MEAL OF THE DAY: EXPECT VELVETY FLAT WHITES, GREEN JUICES AND ACAI BOWLS

So in this tropical mix, it's no surprise to find Artisan Roast's Janszoon blend stocking the grinders, what with its chocolatey notes and fantastically fruity finish and all. Drink it as a long black, or a velvety flat white to see if it really does 'show milk who's boss', as it promises.

Alongside, there are also good lunch options – try the warm wraps served with chunky homemade soups - and check out the gallery which showcases Edinburgh based illustrators' work.

KEY ROASTER
Artisan Roast
Coffee Roasters

BREWING METHOD
Espresso

MACHINE
La Spaziale

GRINDER
Mazzer Major E

OPENING HOURS
Mon-Sun 8am-6pm

 Gluten FREE

 COFFEE BEANS AVAILABLE

 SOYA MILK AVAILABLE

 WIFI

 OUTDOOR seating

 FAMILY FRIENDLY

DISABLED ACCESS

---

www.hulajuicebar.co.uk   T: 0131 2201121

f Hula Juice Bar   🐦 @hulajuicebar   🄾 hulajuicebar

№33. THOMAS J WALLS

35 Forrest Road, Edinburgh, EH1 2QT.

Quite possibly the newest entry in this year's guide – due to open this February 2016 - Thomas J Walls is the latest outlet in the Jon Sharp collection of no-nonsense, espresso based coffee shops.

'Most of the time we say we'll never open another shop, but occasionally something amazing comes up and we can't turn it down,' says Jon.

Easily fitting the "amazing" criteria, this former optician's shop on Forrest Road is virtually unchanged since it was first kitted out by said optician, Mr Walls in the 1930s and is filled with wood panelling, stained glass, marble and bronze. There's even a former stable block out the back. The shop has only changed hands once since then – in the seventies – when it was bought by another optician.

KEY ROASTER
Square Mile
Coffee Roasters

BREWING METHOD
Espresso

MACHINE
Synesso

GRINDER
Mythos

OPENING HOURS
Mon-Fri
7.30am-7pm
Sat-Sun 8am-7pm

INSIDER'S TIP
THE SHOP WAS A BAKERY IN THE 1800S – WHICH EXPLAINS THE BEAUTIFUL BREAD OVEN DOOR TUCKED AWAY IN A CORNER

Creating consistently good quality coffee is the aim at Thomas J Walls, and the team will have the signature Sharp focus on espresso based perfection, using Square Mile along with a series of guest roasters.

And as with all the coffee shops in the set, staff undergo barista training with the man himself – who you may just catch pulling shots behind the counter.

T: 0131 2617582

THE
INDEPENDENT
COFFEE GUIDE SERIES
KNOW WHERE'S GOOD TO GO!

AVAILABLE ONLINE NOW AT
www.indycoffee.guide

NORTHERN COFFEE GUIDE

SCOTTISH COFFEE GUIDE

SOUTH WEST COFFEE GUIDE

34. BREW LAB

6-8 South College Street, Edinburgh, EH8 9AA.

For the speciality coffee geek, Brew Lab is a must-visit in Edinburgh. Not just for über quality coffee served as espresso and pourover, but most especially to experience its nitro cold brew, which has been infused with nitrous oxide for a full, velvety mouthfeel and served on draught, like a glass of creamy stout.

The coffee bar in the Old Town serves a range of meticulously brewed single origin filter, espresso and cold brews which are paired with top notch food of local provenance. And it's this combination, along with the charming location with exposed original stonework and plaster work, that have made it such a fave.

INSIDER'S TIP
A SECOND OUTPOST, IN A CONVERTED GARAGE IN THE WEST END, OPENED IN FEBRUARY

In spring 2015, Dave Law and his team opened their Training Lab, where they teach espresso and filtered brewing techniques to private parties, home baristas and culinary professionals, so everyone can take a little Brew Lab magic home with them.

KEY ROASTER
Has Bean

BREWING METHODS
Espresso, pourover, cold brew

MACHINE
Victoria Arduino VA388 Black Eagle

GRINDER
Nuova Simonelli Mythos One

OPENING HOURS
Mon-Fri 8am-6pm
Sat-Sun 9am-6pm

www.brewlabcoffee.co.uk   T: 0131 6628963
f Brew Lab | Artisan Coffee Bar   @brewlabcoffee   brewlabcoffee

№35. KILIMANJARO COFFEE

104 Nicolson Street, Edinburgh, EH8 9EJ.

Notable for its cheery, bright red exterior, Kilimanjaro's other claim to fame is that it was the very first shop set up in 2004 by double Scottish barista championship winner and all round coffee guru, Jon Sharp.

Inside, there's a nod to its past in the reclaimed furniture and basic fittings – this was a pioneering venture set up on a tight budget.

INSIDER'S TIP DONT BE PUT OFF BY THE QUEUES, IT'S WELL WORTH THE WAIT AND TABLES TURN OVER QUICKLY

Outside, there are a handful of seats, but whether you're grabbing a quick cup or people watching over a coffee, the popularity of Kilimanjaro is evident in both the number and eclectic mix of people you'll find milling around.

In addition to its famed all day breakfasts, a good selection of sandwiches, soups, salads and ciabatta accompany the coffee, which comes from Square Mile – along with guest roasters such as The Barn.

The first of Jon's six coffee shops in the city, Kilimanjaro is an Edinburgh institution and no coffee road trip is complete without calling in.

KEY ROASTER
Square Mile
Coffee Roasters

BREWING METHOD
Espresso

MACHINE
Synesso

GRINDER
Mythos

OPENING HOURS
Mon-Fri
7.30am-8.30pm
Sat-Sun 8am-8pm

COFFEE BEANS AVAILABLE

SOYA MILK AVAILABLE

CYCLE FRIENDLY

OUTDOOR SEATING

DISABLED ACCESS

DOG FRIENDLY

T: 0131 6620135

36. FILAMENT COFFEE

38 Clerk Street, Edinburgh, EH8 9HX.

After a successful pop up on Edinburgh's Victoria Street in 2014, Filament finally found a permanent home on Newington's Clerk Street in May 2015.

Clean white walls, concrete floors and counters and reclaimed wooden tables proclaim its contemporary, speciality coffee ethos, which is complemented by a friendly vibe, chat and great music.

Serving up a constantly rotating selection of single origin coffee from across the globe, filter coffee comes courtesy of a selection roasted by the likes of Square Mile, Workshop and Obadiah, while Has Bean is the Filament house roast for espresso.

INSIDER'S TIP WE CAN TESTIFY TO THE POWER OF THE LEMON AND GINGER SHOT FOR AN AWESOME PICK-ME-UP

As in the decor, they do things in a pared back, simple way and coffee is served "black" "white" or "filter".

Alongside is a good coffee shop menu of fresh juices, cakes and bagels from local favourite, The Bearded Baker, and the Filament fave is a Vegemite and smashed avocado bagel - an Aussie import which has become much loved by the locals.

KEY ROASTER
Has Bean

BREWING METHODS
Espresso,
AeroPress

MACHINE
Nuova Simonelli
Aurelia

GRINDERS
Mythos One, EK43

OPENING HOURS
Mon-Fri
7.30am-7pm
Sat-Sun
9am-7pm

---

www.filamentcoffee.com   T: 0131 2815140

f Filament Coffee   @filamentcoffee   filament_coffee

MAP Nº 37. CULT ESPRESSO

104 Buccleuch Street, Edinburgh, EH8 9NQ.

Don't be mistaken for thinking that this is one of those too-cool-for-school coffee shops, where you need a coffee qualification to get into conversation with the baristas, because this is a cult that everyone's welcome to join.

A fraternal, boyish vibe pervades this tiny little coffee shop - Lego Star Wars figures turn up in the most unexpected places, and you can tell that Kevin, Garry and Drew (father, son and friend) are having a good time slinging coffee and looking after the customers. It's the kind of gaff that we'd all love to run with our mates.

INSIDER'S TIP THE TEAM LIVE IN THE SHOP, SO IF YOU SEE THEM OUT AND ABOUT, PLEASE RETURN THEM

Where they are serious however, is when it comes to speciality coffee. The team has set up their brew bar with Florence (the machine, geddit?) and grinders Bert and Ernie working on the house coffee from Roundhill Roastery, as well as guest beans from the likes of La Cabra, Five Elephants and Horsham Coffee Roasters.

In addition, the gang do good food - simple, seasonal and locally sourced wherever possible. The force is strong with this one.

KEY ROASTER
Round Hill Roastery

BREWING METHODS
Espresso,
AeroPress,
Kalita Wave

MACHINE
Kees van der
Western Mirage
Duetto

GRINDERS
Mythos One, K30

OPENING HOURS
Mon-Fri 8am-6pm
Sat 10am-6pm
Sun 10am-5pm

Gluten FREE

COFFEE BEANS AVAILABLE

SOYA MILK AVAILABLE

WIFI

CYCLE FRIENDLY

OUTDOOR SEATING

DOG FRIENDLY

www.cult-espresso.com   T: 0131 6628083

f Cult Espresso   🐦 @cultcoffeeedin   📷 cult_espresso

38. PRESS COFFEE

30 Buccleuch Street, Edinburgh, EH8 9LP.

This street corner coffee shop on the edge of Edinburgh University campus has two personalities, so what you'll experience depends on the time of day, and the month in which you visit.

During term time, you can join the steady stream of students and lecturers taking time out (or seeking fresh inspiration) in a coffee shop environs. And when the lively hustle and bustle of university life eases into holiday mode, Press transforms into a quiet oasis – which is appropriate considering its closeness to the Meadows public park.

One of the stable of coffee shops belonging to barista champ Jon Sharp, it's no surprise to discover that – in common with all his other venues – there's great loyalty to espresso here.

INSIDER'S TIP THE SPIT ROAST BAKED POTATO SHOP IS IN THE SAME BUILDING AND NO ONE MINDS IF YOU TAKE FOOD AND DRINK BETWEEN THE TWO STORES

The coffee is the foundation of this cafe, and you can expect it to be served with skill and passion by the knowledgeable baristas. There's a selection of breakfast and brunch options to enjoy at this light, airy space which features great artwork.

KEY ROASTER
Square Mile
Coffee Roasters

BREWING METHOD
Espresso

MACHINE
Synesso

GRINDER
Mythos

OPENING HOURS
Mon-Fri 8am-6pm
Sat-Sun 9am-5pm

SOYA MILK AVAILABLE

CYCLE FRIENDLY

OUTDOOR SEATING

DOG FRIENDLY

T: 0131 6676205

№39. SÖDERBERG

1 Lister Square, Edinburgh, EH3 9GL.

C all in to this bakery for a taste of Scandinavia – complete with coffee from Stockholm roaster, Johan & Nyström.

Söderberg has become an Edinburgh institution, with two cafes in Stockbridge and Quartermile, along with bakery shops in the West-End and Quartermile, and a flagship site in the glass North Pavilion, designed by Foster & Partner.

The focus is on honest, artisan goods using first-class ingredients, with a big dose of individuality - whether that's through a baker hand-crafting one of its signature Swedish breakfast buns or a barista pulling a shot.

INSIDER'S TIP TRY THE SALMON BRUNCH PIZZA AND VALRHONA CARDAMOM HOT CHOCOLATE

Staying true to its Scandi heritage, Söderberg sources beans from Johan & Nyström, working with this Swedish coffee roaster in particular for its slow roast profiles. *'The Bella bean is slow-roasted for a more rounded, rich and chocolatey flavour,'* says Clare.

Sample smörrebröd, sourdough pizzas or waffles cooked on the stone oven and admire the trad Scandi furnishings inside, or step outside and watch the team at work in the upper floor bakery, through the floor to ceiling windows.

KEY ROASTER
Johan & Nyström

BREWING METHODS
Espresso, filter

MACHINE
La Marzocco

GRINDER
Mazzer

OPENING HOURS
Mon-Thur 8am-5pm
Fri 8am-10.30pm
Sat 10am-10.30pm
Sun 10am-4pm

COFFEE BEANS AVAILABLE

SOYA MILK AVAILABLE

OUTDOOR SEATING

FAMILY FRIENDLY

DISABLED ACCESS

www.soderberg.uk   T: 0131 2281905

f Söderberg   ⓘ soderbergbakery

MAP No. 40. LEO & TED

36 Leven Street, Edinburgh, EH3 9LJ.

If the quirky "knowledge bombs" scribbled on the chalk board outside Leo & Ted in Tollcross don't draw you in, the glorious smell of freshly ground coffee and home baked cakes certainly will.

Leo & Ted is husband and wife duo, Joe and Marie Denby's second coffee shop in the city. They're already doing their coffee thang over at Leo's Beanery in the New Town - where great coffee meets friendly neighbourhood cafe.

INSIDER'S TIP RUMBLING TUMS SHOULD HEAD TO THE COUNTER, STOCKED WITH BREAKFAST CROISSANTS, GLUTEN FREE BAKES AND HEARTY SOUP

That freshly ground waft which tempted you in is sourced from a range of micro-roasters across the UK, with the house blend, Leo's 80/20 from Hands-On, always available in one of the grinders. If you like what you're tasting, ask one of the knowledgeable baristas to grind it to order so you can take it away to enjoy your latest find at home.

That said, we reckon you'll want to stick around at this cool new coffee hangout. Joe and Marie designed and built the whole place by hand, using reclaimed wood and other recycled materials - the drinks menu is even made from their old sash window.

KEY ROASTER
Hands-On

BREWING METHOD
Espresso

MACHINE
La Marzocco

GRINDERS
Mazzer Super Jolly x2, Mythos One

OPENING HOURS
Mon-Fri 8am-5pm
Sat 9am-5pm
Sun 10am-5pm

---

www.leoandted.co.uk   T: 07500221009

f Leo and Ted   🐦 @leoandted   📷 leoandted

₄41. ARTISAN ROAST BRUNTSFIELD

138 Bruntsfield Place, Edinburgh, EH10 4ER.

S tarting life as a pop up during the 2011 Fringe Festival, Artisan Roast's Bruntsfield venue was such a hit during the comedy fest that it decided to stick around once the laughs had left town.

It quickly gained a reputation as *the* neighbourhood hangout to be seen in and you'll find a welcoming mix of regulars and coffee disciples filling the small but open plan space.

INSIDER'S TIP BOOK AN ESPRESSO MASTERCLASS WITH ONE OF ARTISAN ROAST'S BAD-ASS BARISTAS

There's a team of young baristas operating the La Marzocco machine, eager to chat about brewing methods and bean varieties as they craft the perfect cup – so prepare to be patient as good coffee takes time.

A coffee shop not a cafe, don't expect a comprehensive dining menu, but stop by around lunchtime for good avocado on toasted sourdough and hot homemade soup.

KEY ROASTER
Artisan Roast Coffee Roasters

BREWING METHODS
Espresso, Kalita Wave, AeroPress, Chemex

MACHINE
La Marzocco FB80

GRINDERS
Mahlkonig K30, Mazzer Major Electronic

OPENING HOURS
Mon-Fri
8am-6.30pm
Sat-Sun
9am-6pm

www.artisanroast.co.uk   **T:** 07475796474

f Artisan Roast Bruntsfield   🐦 @artisanroast   📷 artisanroast

MAP Nº 42. PROJECT COFFEE

192-194 Bruntsfield Place, Edinburgh, EH10 4DF.

Very much a part of the Bruntsfield Place neighbourhood, this is somewhere to hang out and people-watch, so it's just as well that Project has huge picture windows (and outdoor tables for fresh air types) to enhance the experience.

Over the last five to 10 years this area has seen the growth of a number of independent shops and cafes, and Project is firmly positioned among them, serving beautifully made scones (all baked on the premises of course), sandwiches and brunches. In fact, coffee and breakfast at the weekend has become a bit of an institution with the locals.

INSIDER'S TIP
GET THERE EARLY ON SATURDAYS – IT GETS SUPER BUSY FOR BRUNCH

Project is one of a collection of six shops in the city owned by Jon Sharp, although you'd be hard pushed to spot any similarities between them all. Every shop is different, getting its character from the building, neighbourhood and customers who visit. What does remain the same though is a commitment to serving a perfect, espresso-based coffee with all staff training done by Jon himself. *'We put all our energy in to getting one thing perfect,'* he says.

KEY ROASTER
Square Mile
Coffee Roasters

BREWING METHOD
Espresso

MACHINE
Synesso

GRINDER
Mythos

OPENING HOURS
Mon-Fri
7.30am-7pm
Sat-Sun 8am-6pm

COFFEE BEANS AVAILABLE

SOYA MILK AVAILABLE

CYCLE FRIENDLY

OUTDOOR SEATING

FAMILY FRIENDLY

DISABLED ACCESS

DOG FRIENDLY

T: 0131 2296758

ᴹᴬᴾ ᴺᵒ **43. BLACKWOOD COFFEE**

235 Morningside Road, Edinburgh, EH10 4QT.

There's plenty of space in this light filled street corner coffee shop situated among Morningside's collection of boutique shops.

It's restful and elegant inside, with little brass topped, round wooden tables filling the panelled room.

While there's a more traditional atmosphere than you'd find in most urban coffee shops, the coffee is just as technically spot on and expertly delivered. Not surprising then to learn that Blackwood is one of barista champ Jon Sharp's collection, with his signature all-espresso-based drinks using beans from Square Mile along with guest roasters.

INSIDER'S TIP GO FOR THE BLACKWOOD BREAKFAST – POACHED EGGS, BACON, ASPARAGUS AND HOLLANDAISE SAUCE

A good selection of bites to eat includes scones baked in the shop every morning which are a hit with the regulars.

Maybe Blackwood's interior is a nod to Jon's childhood coffee inspiration. *'When I was young my mum took me to cafes for coffee,'* he says, *'and she'd comment on whether it was good or bad and I'd ask her the reasons why ... it's always stuck in my mind.'* His subsequent quest for coffee perfection is what led to his six Edinburgh shops, including this essential stop off.

KEY ROASTER
Square Mile
Coffee Roasters

BREWING METHOD
Espresso

MACHINE
Synesso

GRINDER
Mythos

OPENING HOURS
Mon-Fri 8am-6pm
Sat 9am-6pm
Sun 9am-5pm

T: 0131 4460429

44. GREENSHOOTS

6-8 Alexander Drive, Gorgie, Edinburgh, EH11 2RH.

reating a welcoming and unpretentious space where expertly brewed coffee meets wholesome, locally sourced food, the team at Greenshoots has struck the perfect balance between coffee house geekery and neighbourhood cafe.

A newcomer to the Edinburgh coffee scene, owner Lynn Gatherer is proud to be the first in the region to serve Charlie Mills ethically sourced and expertly roasted coffee. Alongside the micro-roasted house coffee and seasonal blends pulled through the espresso machine, there are also stunning single origin beans for V60 pourovers - make sure to ask one of the friendly baristas for the day's tasting notes.

INSIDER'S TIP WORK YOUR WAY THROUGH THE SINGLE ORIGIN POUROVERS FOR A UNIQUE COFFEE EXPERIENCE EACH VISIT

Coffee alternatives include loose leaf teas and locally brewed soft drinks such as Kitsch's rhubarb and Thai basil soda, plus there's an intriguing selection of open sandwiches and cakes. And along with your coffee-to-go, you can also take away some fabulous homewares and gifts, selected to showcase leading craftsmen, designers and artists from around the UK.

KEY ROASTER
Charlie Mills Coffee

BREWING METHODS
Espresso, V60, filter

MACHINE
Rocket Boxer

GRINDER
Mahlkonig EK-43 Copper

OPENING HOURS
Mon closed
Tue-Fri 9am-5pm
Sat 9.30am-5pm
Sun 10.30am-4.30pm

Gluten FREE

COFFEE BEANS AVAILABLE

SOYA MILK AVAILABLE

WIFI

CYCLE FRIENDLY

OUTDOOR seating

FAMILY friendly

COFFEE COURSES AVAILABLE

DISABLED ACCESS

DOG FRIENDLY

www.greenshootsedinburgh.com   T: 0131 2617323
f Greenshoots   @greenshootsedin   greenshootsedinburgh

MORE GOOD CUPS

So many cool places to drink coffee ...

45. THE CEILIDH PLACE

14 West Argyle Street, Ullapool, IV26 2TY.

www.theceilidhplace.com

T: 01854 612103

f The Ceilidh Place
🐦 @theceilidhplace

46. WINDRUSH CAFE STUDIO

Struan, Isle of Skye, IV56 8FB.

www.morbooks.co.uk

T: 01470 572782

f Mòr Books & the Windrush Cafe Studio
🐦 @windrushcafe

47. CAFE SIA

Broadford, Isle of Skye, IV49 9AB.

www.cafesia.co.uk

T: 01471 822616

f Cafesiaskye
🐦 @skyecoffee
📷 cafesia_skye

48. THE BAKEHOUSE

Old Quay, Mallaig, PH41 4QF.

T: 01687 462808

f The Bakehouse
🐦 @mallaigbakes
📷 mallaigbakes

49. PAPERCUP COFFEE COMPANY

603 Great Western Road, Glasgow, G12 8HX.

www.papercupcoffeecompany.bigcartel.com

T: 07719454376

f Papercup Coffee Company
🐦 @pccoffeeuk
📷 pccoffeeuk

50. SIEMPRE

162 Dumbarton Road, Glasgow, G11 6XE.

www.siemprebicyclecafe.com

T: 0141 3342385

f Siempre Bicycle Cafe
🐦 @siemprecafebar
📷 siemprebicyclecafe

51. THE STEAMIE

1024 Argyle Street, Glasgow, G3 8LX.

www.thesteamie.co.uk

f The Steamie
🐦 @the_steamie
📷 thesteamie

52. COFFEE CHOCOLATE AND TEA

944 Argyle Street, Glasgow, G3 8YJ.

www.coffeechocolateandtea.com

T: 0141 2043161

f CC&T Coffee Chocolate and Tea
🐦 @roasteryglasgow
📷 roasteryglasgow

53. RIVERHILL COFFEE BAR
24 Gordon Street, Glasgow, G1 3PU.

www.riverhillcafe.com

T: 0141 2044762

f Riverhill Coffee Bar
🐦 @riverhillcoffee
📷 riverhill_coffeebar

54. BAKERY47
76 Victoria Road, Glasgow, G42 7AA.

www.bakery47.com

T: 0141 2379470

f Bakery47
🐦 @bakery47
📷 bakery47

55. COFFEE ON WOOER
2-4 Wooer Street, Falkirk, FK1 1NJ.

www.coffeeonwooer.co.uk

T: 01324 278026

f Coffee On Wooer
🐦 @cowfalkirk
📷 cowfalkirk

56. DIGGORY'S
63-64 High Street, Haddington,
East Lothian, EH41 3ED.

www.diggorys.co.uk

T: 07792252012

f Diggory's
🐦 @diggorys_coffee
📷 diggorys

57. GAMMA TRANSPORT DIVISION
6 Dean Park Street, Stockbridge,
Edinburgh, EH4 1JW.

www.gammatransportdivision.com

T: 0131 3321777

f Gamma Transport Division
🐦 @transdivision
📷 gammatd

58. SÖDERBERG CAFE
3 Deanhaugh Street, Edinburgh, EH4 1LU.

www.soderberg.uk

T: 0131 3322901

f Söderberg
📷 soderbergbakery

59. RONDE
66-68 Hamilton Place, Stockbridge,
Edinburgh, EH3 5AZ.

www.rondebike.com

T: 0131 2609888

f Ronde - Bicycle Outfitters
🐦 @rondebike
📷 rondebike

60. PEP & FODDER
11 Waterloo Place, Edinburgh, EH1 3BG.

www.pepandfodder.com

T: 0131 5565119

f Pep & Fodder
🐦 @pepfodder
📷 pepandfodder

61. SÖDERBERG BAKERY SHOP
31 Queensferry Street, Edinburgh, EH2 4QS.

www.soderberg.uk

T: 0131 2258286

f Söderberg
📷 soderbergbakery

62. LOVECRUMBS
155 West Port, Edinburgh, EH3 9DP.

www.lovecrumbs.co.uk

T: 0131 6290626

f Lovecrumbs
🐦 @hellolovecrumbs
📷 hellolovecrumbs

63. THE COUNTER - TOLLCROSS

Police Box, High Riggs, Tollcross, EH3 9RP.

f The Counter
🐦 @thecountered
📷 thecountered

64. MACHINA ESPRESSO

2 Brougham Place, Tollcross, Edinburgh, EH3 9HW.

www.machina-espresso.co.uk

T: 0131 2293495

f Machina Espresso
🐦 @machinaespresso
📷 machinaespresso

65. PEKOETEA

20 Leven Street, Edinburgh, EH3 9LJ.

www.pekoetea.co.uk

T: 0131 4771838

f PekoeTea
🐦 @pekoetea
📷 pekoetea_edinburgh

66. BEARDED BARISTA

East Crichton Street, Edinburgh, EH8 9AB.

🐦 @beardedbarista_

67. SÖDERBERG BAKERY SHOP

Quartermile, 33 Simpson Loan, Edinburgh, EH3 9GG.

www.soderberg.uk

T: 0131 2285876

f Söderberg
📷 soderbergbakery

68. SÖDERBERG CAFE

Quartermile, 27 Simpson Loan,Edinburgh, EH3 9GG.

www.soderberg.uk

T: 0131 2285876

f Söderberg
📷 soderbergbakery

69. COBOLT COFFEE

Police Box, Marchmont Crescent, Edinburgh, EH9 1HL.

f Cobolt Coffee
🐦 @coboltcoffee
📷 coboltcoffee

70. SALT CAFE

54-56 Morningside Road, Edinburgh, EH10 4BZ.

T: 0131 2811885

f Salt Café
🐦 @saltmorningside
📷 salt_cafe_morningside

71. THE COUNTER - MORNINGSIDE

Police Box, 216a Morningside Road, Edinburgh, EH10 4QQ.

f The Counter
🐦 @thecountered
📷 thecountered

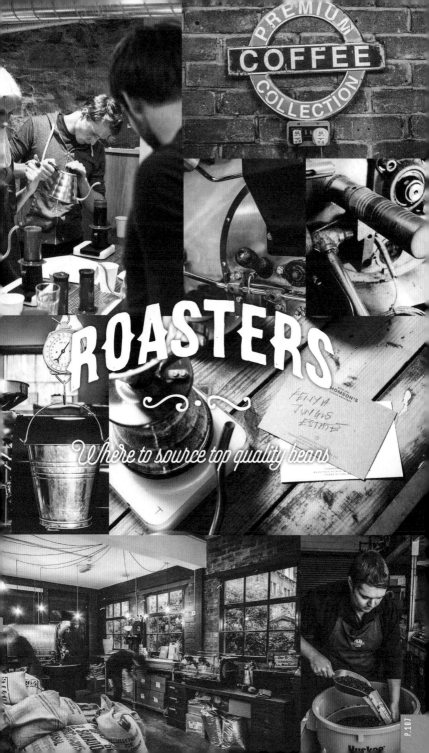

PREMIUM COFFEE COLLECTION

ROASTERS

Where to source top quality beans

№72. HOME GROUND COFFEE

Lyleston West Lodge, Cardross, Dumbarton, Argyll and Bute, G82 5HF.
www.homegroundcoffee.co.uk   T: 01389 841730

f Home Ground Coffee   🐦 @the_coffee_guy

There can't be many coffee bods who can match the passion, dogged determination and inventiveness of Alastair Moodie. Starting out around six years ago – with no money – he encountered numerous setbacks, the like of which would send all but the toughest roaster running.

The venture started as a hobby when an old telephone exchange which backed on to his garden went up for sale. *'It cost peanuts,'* says Alastair, *'but took months to get sorted as a very small roastery.'*

'WITHIN A YEAR HE WAS AT LATITUDE FESTIVAL SERVING COFFEE FROM A MULTI POUROVER COFFEE MAKER'

Alastair built his own 1kg roaster and set about experimenting - although everything seemed to go against him (planning problems, con artists and a global recession to name but a few of the issues). But then he met a chap at a Loch Lomond farmers' market, and became involved in the Food From Argyle network.

He started going to events to try and make money from the coffee he was roasting, and within a year was at Latitude with a multi pourover coffee maker that allowed him to brew 16 cups at one time - *'I build what I can't afford,'* he says.

It seems Alastair has always been ahead of the game - serving both pourover and cold brew at festivals, *'eons before it became cool'.*

Later he was able to upgrade to a 30 year old Probat LP5, but all the roasting still takes place in the exchange.

Nowadays Alastair specialises in bespoke blends for cafes, restaurants and hotels, introducing them, through training, to the world of speciality coffee. *'It's the people who grow it, where it's grown, the history behind it – you never stop learning,'* he says.

His biggest gig was supplying coffee to the Commonwealth Games. *'It's certainly been a crazy few years, and taken blood, sweat and tears to get where we are now'* he says, reflecting, with some amazement, on his roller coaster coffee journey.

COFFEE BEANS AVAILABLE ONLINE

COFFEE COURSES AVAILABLE

73. AVENUE COFFEE ROASTING CO.

321 Great Western Road, Glasgow, G4 9HR.
www.avenue.coffee   T: 0141 3870249

f Avenue Coffee   @avenue_coffee   avenuecoffeeglasgow

Starting life as a speciality coffee shop, Avenue Coffee Roasting Co. was created with a very specific aim, *'to make the best coffee and share it with as many people as possible'*. But just grinding and brewing the stuff didn't quite cut it for general manager, Todd Whiteford or his team at the Glasgow cafe.

So, when the purchase of a second venue gave the team more room, it was a natural step to invest in a Diedrich IR-12 roaster.

'Roasting our own coffee was always part of the plan,' explains Todd. *'It seemed logical to start one step further back in the chain, and to produce the best quality coffee. When we purchased the second premises there was space for a little roasting lab and we thought, why not?'*

Freshers in the roasting world, Avenue is still making a name for itself, stocking the grinders in its own cafes along with a small selection of artisan shops across the UK. *'There's a huge halo effect around roasting, people will often see a name and stick to it, plus we've got some tough competition in a city like Glasgow,'* says Todd, *'but we encourage our customers to visit on Mondays and Wednesdays and grill the roasters as they work!'*

'THERE WAS SPACE FOR A LITTLE ROASTING LAB AND WE THOUGHT, WHY NOT?'

Offering training to all of its wholesale customers, as well as brew nights and cupping events in the cafes, the tight-knit team is working hard to make Avenue stand out, and as Todd says, *'the competition may be pretty good, but we believe in our product, and that's what counts.'*

MAP.№ 74. DEAR GREEN COFFEE ROASTERS

Unit 2, 13-27 East Campbell Street, Glasgow, G1 5DT.
www.deargreencoffee.com   T: 0141 5527774

f Dear Green Coffee Roasters   🐦 @coffeeglasgow   📷 deargreen

I f you can pin Lisa Lawson of Dear Green down long enough, you'll discover she's a whirlwind of enthusiasm for speciality coffee in Scotland and a groundbreaker in her own right.

'We are proud to be the first roastery in Glasgow to only roast speciality coffee, and originally set up to bring seasonal, speciality grade coffee to a city which had a limited coffee culture,' she says. *'We started roasting on a shoestring in a tiny room, and cycled around Glasgow with our deliveries.'*

Dear Green (set up in Lisa's home city and the Gaelic translation of Glasgow) is still a small company, but punches above its weight in terms of quality.

'SET UP IN LISA'S HOME CITY, DEAR GREEN IS THE GAELIC TRANSLATION OF "GLASGOW"'

Lisa's own coffee journey began while working for an Aussie roaster in the early noughties, and since then, her work in Scotland has included the set up of the roastery, getting involved in the launch of a number of leading coffee shops such as Laboratorio Espresso

and Riverhill, and the creation of Glasgow Coffee Festival and the Scottish AeroPress Championships. Indeed, you often hear remarks like, *'if Lisa's involved, it'll be good'.*

COFFEE BEANS AVAILABLE ONLINE

Sourcing beans from across the globe through speciality green bean importers, as well as forging direct trade links to quality coffee farms, you'll find Dear Green beans at top notch coffee shops across the country. And as part of her commitment to ethical sourcing and education, Lisa travels to visit farms wherever possible.

With an innovator at the helm, Dear Green has all the bases covered, selling to home baristas as well as wholesale from the centrally based roastery, offering barista training and cupping events, and selling coffee online. *'In short, we are committed to quality, flavour and a sustainable industry with ethical practices throughout the supply chain,'* she says with a smile.

75. OVENBIRD COFFEE ROASTERS

Block B, Unit 2, 45 Glenwood Place, Glasgow, G45 9UH.

www.ovenbird.co.uk   T: 0141 6340309

f Ovenbird Coffee Roasters   🐦 @ovenbird_coffee   📷 ovenbird_coffee

Even the name, Ovenbird Coffee Roasters, is rooted in the traditional African coffee farms where its owner David Angeletti once lived and worked.

The ovenbird is a migratory songbird which takes refuge in the heavily shaded coffee farms; it helps African farmers by being an extremely efficient and motivated insect-pest controller.

And, like the ovenbird, David's story covers thousands of miles.

It was while working at a traditional roastery in Italy (in order to pay his way through an archaeology and history degree) that he first became interested in coffee. Realising that it was coffee and not archaeology that held his future, he moved to Africa after graduating to work with farmers and help them increase their coffee yields, process coffee and build new processing plants - roasting and selling the beans into Europe and America.

After seven years in Africa, David needed a new challenge and to grow his coffee knowledge, so he migrated to the UK, where, after consulting and roasting in London, he and his family built a nest in Scotland.

Inspired by the people and landscape of Africa, and intrigued by lighter roasting methods which bring out the characteristics of the beans, David decided to open his own roasting business.

'LIKE THE OVENBIRD, DAVID'S STORY COVERS THOUSANDS OF MILES'

Ovenbird focuses on single origin beans and their specific flavours, such as the citrus notes from Rwandan beans, or the malty, whisky flavours of Kenyan peaberry.

David's approach is very artisan, relying on sight, sound and experience to roast coffee, and – instead of developing a specific style of roasting – he concentrates on, *'developing flavours that are an expression of the farm, the country and environment in which the coffee was grown.*

'I want to tell the story of the coffee alongside the people who produce it,' he says, *'because I want it to reflect the landscape, the people and the feeling of actually being there.'*

COFFEE BEANS AVAILABLE ONLINE

COFFEE COURSES AVAILABLE

MAP No. 76. THOMSON'S COFFEE ROASTERS

Burnfield Avenue, Glasgow, G46 7TL.
www.thomsonscoffee.com   T: 0141 6370683

f Thomsons Coffee   🐦 @thomsonscoffee   📷 thomsonscoffee

The true pioneers of speciality coffee in Scotland, Thomson's Coffee Roasters has been going strong for a whopping 175 years – and there's no sign that this family run business is planning on retiring any time soon.

Founded in 1841 by tea and coffee merchant David Thomson, the company has supplied speciality coffee to the people of Scotland through many guises over the past century, before opening its first roastery in 1960, on Glasgow's south side. Over 50 years later, Thomson's still calls the same custom built roastery home.

COFFEE BEANS AVAILABLE SOLD ON SITE **& ONLINE**

COFFEE COURSES AVAILABLE

Inside the building, technology honours this tradition, with two antique Whitmee flame roasters used alongside Scotland's first state-of-the art Loring Smart roaster to create an extensive range of single origin, small batch, organic and original blends.

Conversely, home baristas can source all manner of gear required to produce the perfect brew on its website.

Being in the coffee business this long certainly has its advantages, and when it comes to importing the best quality beans, having over 40 years of strong trade relationships in the bag definitely comes in handy.

'THOMSON'S COFFEE ROASTERS HAS BEEN GOING STRONG FOR A WHOPPING 175 YEARS'

Keeping up with the changing face of artisan roasting, Thomson's is also developing direct trade relationships with a number of small producers in Peru, Rwanda and Ecuador, which promise to deliver some delicious and innovative coffees.

Photos: Gavin Smart Photography www.viewfromtheoutside.net

77. GLEN LYON COFFEE ROASTERS

Aberfeldy Business Park, Dunkeld Road, Aberfeldy, Perthshire, PH15 2AQ.

www.glenlyoncoffee.co.uk   T: 01887 822817

f Glen Lyon Coffee   🐦 @glenlyoncoffee   📷 glenlyoncoffee

'I love the international side of coffee,' says Fiona Grant of Glen Lyon Coffee Roasters in Aberfeldy.

Indeed it was working as a journalist in Bolivia that she met her husband and business partner-to-be Jamie, and caught the coffee bug. *'Coffee was my passion,'* she says, *'and it wasn't long before Jamie fell for it too'.*

However, it was a few years later, and after they'd returned to Scotland and had their son Tom, that Jamie gave up his job in conservation so they could take a family trip down the west coast of the States to visit some American micro roasteries. *'Inspiration struck as we realised that we could do that in the Highlands,'* Fiona says, *'and it turned out that Jamie has a natural talent for roasting.'*

Five years on they've built a respected roastery with a team of four, cooking up beans in their 12kg Probat, and selling mainly in the Highlands.

'INSPIRATION STRUCK AS WE REALISED THAT WE COULD DO THAT IN THE HIGHLANDS'

Jamie and Fiona's wanderlust is sated through their day to day interaction with beans from across the globe, sourced through importer Mercanta (*'we can trace our coffee all the way to the individual farmers who grew it'*), as well as through trips out to origin. Fiona recently hit the coffee trail to Rwanda, and has plans to take Tom to Colombia next year.

Visiting the farms has further developed the team's commitment to social responsibility and environmental practices, *'and we are proud to pay our producers substantially over Fair Trade prices for their amazing beans.'*

COFFEE BEANS AVAILABLE
SOLD ON SITE & ONLINE

№78. THE BEAN SHOP

67 George Street, Perth, PH1 5LB.
www.thebeanshop.co.uk   T: 01738 449955

f The Bean Shop   🐦 @thebeanshopuk   📷 thebeanshopuk

The good people of Perth are extremely lucky to have on tap such an eclectic range of coffees and teas from around the world.

Since 2003, John and Lorna Bruce have been roasting in the basement - using a 5kg Probat, and more recently a Loring Falcon - to stock their seductive little shop with coffees alongside a plethora of teas.

Beans come from their direct relationships with farms in Honduras and Peru, as well as those sourced from other coffee growing areas. *The range is all about getting customers to expand their horizons,'* says Lorna, *'which is why we offer wee tasters of coffee all day, every day'.*

Quality and hand crafting are the watch words here, and everything sold is roasted in small batches with the aim of bringing out the natural characteristics of the bean. It's then sold on the same day or the day after.

'THE RANGE IS ALL ABOUT GETTING CUSTOMERS TO EXPAND THEIR HORIZONS, WHICH IS WHY WE OFFER WEE TASTERS OF COFFEE ALL DAY EVERY DAY'

John was brought up on a tea plantation in Darjeeling, while Lorna has been roasting since the late 1990s when, as an art student in Aberdeen she started working at one of Scotland's first indie roasters, MacBeans. The tradition and family connection continues as they raise their own two boys while building the business.

If you can't visit to pick up your beans, sign up for the monthly six or 12 month subscription and get it delivered.

COFFEE BEANS AVAILABLE SOLD ON SITE & ONLINE

COFFEE COURSES AVAILABLE

MAP No. 79. LUCKIE BEANS

Love Lane, Berwick Upon Tweed, Northumberland, TD15 1AR.
www.luckiebeans.co.uk   T: 07810446537

🐦 @luckiebeans   📷 luckie_beans

Jamie McLuckie may have only been roasting since April 2015, but it was by no means pot luck that the Luckie Beans founder scooped fifth place at the first UK Coffee Roasting Championships – pipping the very roasters who inspired him to join the trade.

Hooked since the age of three (seriously), coffee's always been a big interest for Jamie, but only recently has it become his career.

For years he travelled the world working in the music industry, *'I saw some amazing coffee shops while travelling with my job,'* he explains, *'so I witnessed how different cultures use coffee in different ways.'* Then last year, when his wife became pregnant, Jamie decided to give coffee a shot.

'GET FRESHLY ROASTED BEANS DELIVERED TO YOUR DOOR FROM SINGULAR BAGS TO MONTLY SUBSCRIPTIONS'

Roasting in small batches on a Diedrich IR2.5 at the HQ in Berwick Upon Tweed, Luckie

Beans is all about attention to detail. *'We're not churning out coffee for the sake of it,'* says Jamie, *'we take time to make the coffee the best it can be.'*

COFFEE BEANS AVAILABLE ONLINE

Over the past couple of months, the team has been working hard to create a signature Love Lane house blend, named after the street it calls home, as well as exciting single origin offerings such as the rare La Esperanza Cerro Azul Geisha, with notes of blueberry, passion fruit and sweet chocolate.

The small group of cafes serving Luckie Beans is slowly growing, while home baristas can take out a subscription to get a regular supply of freshly roasted beans delivered to their door.

They say you make your own luck, and with all of this under his belt in less than a year, McLuckie's clearly working hard at it.

№80. STEAMPUNK COFFEE

49a Kirk Ports, North Berwick, East Lothian, EH39 4HL.
www.steampunkcoffee.co.uk   T: 01620 893030 (cafe no.)

f Steampunk Coffee   🐦 @steampunkcoffee   📷 steampunkcoffee

Photos: Gavin Smart Photography www.viewfromtheoutside.net

Steampunk Coffee has been roasting in North Berwick since 2012. Having begun small-scale in a garage, it expanded into a large warehouse in the centre of the pretty seaside town near Edinburgh.

The warehouse is home to both the roastery and a cafe, and visitors can enjoy different Steampunk coffees which are showcased as espresso or filter. It's a hub of activity with roasting happening most weekdays – along with packing. Customers hanging out at the bar get to watch the whole process while enjoying a coffee and indulging in some awesome home baking.

'OUR ROASTS AIM TO SHOWCASE THE ORIGIN IN THE CUP'

The team works hard to source coffee beans as directly and traceably as possible, passing this information on to customers. Working closely with Nordic Approach and Falcon Speciality in sourcing, the team also aims to make lasting links with farmers. And,

having met one of its Colombian growers, there are plans to travel to origin regularly to strengthen those connections.

'As coffee roasters, our aim is to draw out the subtle nuances of flavour in each bean,' says owner Catherine Franks. 'Our roasts unlock each coffee's potential and showcase the origin in the cup. That's why we don't roast for different brew methods or blend beans.'

This is an unusual philosophy in the UK, and as fans of playing around with different brew methods, they believe if a roast is well developed it can be enjoyed prepared in many ways. So they regularly swap the beans they use as espresso and filter in the cafe to illustrate the point.

A passionate commitment to quality, coupled with a strong focus on ethical sourcing results in an interesting and constantly varying offer of coffees from around the globe.

COFFEE BEANS AVAILABLE SOLD ON SITE & ONLINE

MAP N° 81. MR EION COFFEE ROASTER

9 Dean Park Street, Stockbridge, Edinburgh, EH4 1JN.

www.mreion.com   T: 0131 3431354

f Mr. Eion: Coffee Roaster   🐦 @mr_eion   📷 mr_eion

Photos: Gavin Smart Photography www.viewfromtheoutside.net

Behind the unassuming little shopfront in Edinburgh's Stockbridge, you'll find hessian sacks full of green beans from all corners of the world piled up against reclaimed scaffolding beams. And the heart of the operation – a 5kg Diedrich – stands proudly at the back, in full view of visitors.

Eion Henderson describes his roastery as *'a sweetie shop for caffeinated grown ups'*, and it's easy to see why the locals have embraced it.

'IT'S WILD, SO FROM A BIODIVERSITY ASPECT AND FLAVOUR PROFILE ITS A LOT CLOSER TO THE FIRST COFFEES EVER TASTED'

Previously in Aberdeen, Eion has more than a decade of experience in the coffee industry, with a defining moment being a year spent in New York in 2003. It brought him back to Scotland, *'enthused and energised with the whole specialist coffee idea'*.

Having been both a barista and manager, since December 2013 he's bowed out of front of house duties to fully immerse himself in roasting. *'The science really fascinates me. It's the control, how those little variances can make so much difference to the end product, that's so fascinating,'* he says.

COFFEE BEANS AVAILABLE SOLD ON SITE

Roasting and sharing rare micro-lot coffees is a constant delight, like Blueberry Candy from Nicaragua, 121 Project Peruvian Pan de Arbol grown by Samuel Chinchay Calderon, and the latest, an Ethiopian coffee from the forests of the Maji Bench region. Growing in the wild and hand picked, only three bags were produced – and Eion had two of them. *'It's wild, so from a biodiversity aspect and flavour profile it's a lot closer to the first coffees ever tasted. I had a real eureka moment when I first tasted it. And as a roaster, there's a responsibility to make sure that what I do represents all the work that has gone before - right back to the growers.'*

№82. ARTISAN ROAST COFFEE ROASTERS

Unit 4 Kings Haugh Road, Edinburgh, Scotland, EH16 5UY.

www.artisanroast.co.uk T: 07514167470

f Artisan Roast ✪ @artisanroast ☑ artisan_roast

When Chilean Gustavo Pardo and Kiwi Michael Wilson met in Edinburgh, it was no surprise that the pair bonded over shared frustrations of the lack of good coffee in the city – hailing as they do from two of the world's best coffee destinations and all.

Fed up and craving a decent cup, the duo decided to take their coffee fate into their own hands, setting up Scotland's first speciality roastery and cafe, Artisan Roast, in 2007.

Eight years on and they've moved to a bigger home to cater for the increasing demand for artisan coffee, and launched two more cafes in the city, along with an outpost in Glasgow.

Artisan Roast isn't short of an award or two either, and last year it received the Glenfiddich Spirit of Scotland award for outstanding contribution to the Scottish food scene.

'We want to offer people diversity,' explains Gustavo, and roasting on a one of kind, custom built Diedrich roaster is one of Artisan's secret weapons: *'we change our roasting approach in*

every product to keep its taste unique'. Its jet-setting head roaster John Thompson, is the other.

'We also work with a range of single origins to produce distinct coffee roasts,' continues Gustavo, *'with John visiting coffee producers around the world a number of times a year'.* This is to source great coffee from the farmers as well as to help make the whole roasting process more transparent.

'LAST YEAR IT RECEIVED THE GLENFIDDICH SPIRIT OF SCOTLAND AWARD FOR OUTSTANDING CONTRIBUTION TO THE SCOTTISH FOOD SCENE'

You'll find Artisan Roast's quirky range of coffees in cafes all over Scotland and the rest of the UK, while it sells beans and coffee equipment from the website – and offers espresso masterclasses too.

-8 South College Street, Edinburgh, EH8 9AA.
vww.brewlabcoffee.co.uk/training   T: 0131 6628963
Brew Lab | Artisan Coffee Bar   🐦 @brewlabcoffee   ⬚ brewlabcoffee

A n invitation down to the basement isn't something we'd usually accept, but when it comes to Brew Lab in Edinburgh, an exception must be made. The speciality coffee shop on South College Street is a popular spot or good coffee and tasty grub, but it's also harbouring a wonderfully geeky lair under ts floorboards.

Kitted out with all the latest coffee tech, ncluding a custom built brew bar and a fully functioning espresso set up – featuring its super sleek Slayer machine, this is where many of Edinburgh's baristas have learned their trade.

Owners David Law and Tom Hyde offer a ange of coffee courses, from introductory essons for the complete coffee novice, to ilter brewing and espresso masterclasses or professional and home baristas looking to orush up their skills.

The specially tailored courses are held in small groups to ensure every student gets the most out of the experience, and there are also bespoke private sessions with Brew Lab's head barista for enthusiasts wanting to hone in on a particular aspect of coffee making.

COFFEE COURSES AVAILABLE

'IF YOU'RE PREPPING FOR A COMPETITION, YOU CAN HIRE THE TRAINING LAB TO MASTER YOUR TECHNIQUE IN PRIVATE'

If you're prepping for a competition, you can hire the lab to master your technique in private. Meanwhile, head barista, Emiliya, hosts coffee training sessions in cafes across Scotland, for businesses wanting to up their brewing game.

MORE GOOD ROASTERS

84. SKYE ROASTERY

Cafe Sia, Broadford, Isle of Skye, IV49 9AB.

www.cafesia.co.uk

T: 01471 822616

f Cafesiaskye
🐦 @skyecoffee
📷 cafesia_skye

85. MACBEANS

2 Little Belmont Street, Aberdeen, AB10 1JG.

www.macbeans.com

T: 01224 624757

f MacBeans Coffee & Tea
🐦 @macbeanscoffee
📷 macbeans

86. PAPERCUP COFFEE COMPANY

603 Great Western Road, Glasgow, G12 8HX.

www.papercupcoffeecompany.bigcartel.com

T: 07719454376

f Papercup Coffee Company
🐦 @pccoffeeuk
📷 pccoffeeuk

87. TAPA COFFEE

721 Pollokshaws Road, Strathbungo, Glasgow, G41 2AA.

www.tapacoffee.com

T: 0141 4239494

f Tapa organic
🐦 @tapaorganic
📷 tapaorganic

88. CHARLIE MILLS COFFEE

Eaglesham, Glasgow, G76 0BB.

www.charliemillscoffee.com

T: 07944667880

f Charlie Mills Coffee
🐦 @cmcoffeeroaster
📷 charliemillscoffee

89. ROUNDSQUARE ROASTERY

Unit 4, Lorne Arcade, 115 High Street, Ayr, KA7 1QL.

www.roundsquareroastery.co.uk

T: 01292 618657

f Roundsquare Roastery
🐦 @roundsquareayr
📷 roundsquarecoffeeroastery

90. SACRED GROUNDS COFFEE COMPANY

Unit 15, Arbroath Business Centre, Dens Road, Arbroath, DD11 1RS.

www.sacredgroundscoffeecompany.co.uk

f Sacred Grounds Coffee Company
🐦 @sacredgrounds14
📷 sacred_grounds_coffee_company

BREW
GLOSSARY

**STRUGGLING TO KEEP UP WITH THE
BREW METHODS AND TERMINOLOGY?
HERE'S THE LOWDOWN ON THE LINGO ...**

AEROPRESS

A syringe-shaped filter brew method that includes an element of mechanical extraction with the water being forced through the coffee and filter paper.

ALTO AIR

An open-sided conical brewer, adaptable to many filter papers such as V60, Melitta or Kalita.

CAFETIERE

Also known as the french press. A coarse metal filter is plunged through coffee grounds which are immersed in water. High on body with characteristic residue in the bottom of the cup afterwards.

CHEMEX

A classic jug/filter combination invented in the fifties, the Chemex is both brew method and serving jug in one. It has circular or square filter papers characterised by the method of folding, leaving three sheets on one side and one on the other.

CLEVER DRIPPER

Essentially a Melitta cone with a fancy bottom plate, you can brew with full immersion until you place the brewer on your cup or jug, then lift the bottom plate and allow the brewed coffee to drain out.

COLD BREW

Coffee brewed cold as opposed to brewed hot and then chilled, either through an immersion method or a tower, where the water drips slowly through the coffee bed.

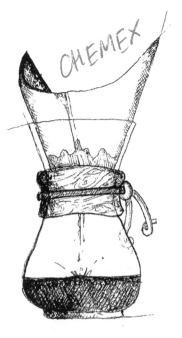

DRIP/BATCH BREWERS

Very similar in principle to pourovers, and more likely found in high volume cafes. They have a showerhead instead of one stream of water and varying degrees of automation. Some will use paper filters and others fine mesh. The key thing with bulk brewing, though, is to always check on the hold time, because the coffee can quickly lose its volatile compounds (they give it that wonderful smell) leaving a baked or metallic flavour note.

EK SHOTS/COFFEE SHOTS

Originating from a Barista Championships performance, the EK refers to Mahlkonig's EK43 grinder which has taken the cafe world by storm. Essentially a lungo (long shot of espresso) made on the espresso machine but giving a considerably better cup of coffee than the lungo which was often characterised by over-extracted bitterness.

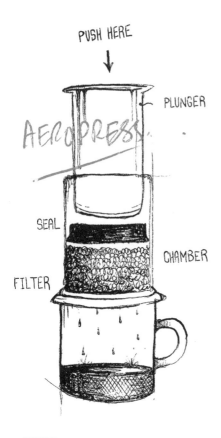

PUSH HERE

AEROPRESS

PLUNGER

SEAL

CHAMBER

FILTER

KALITA

A manufacturer of pourover filters, generally referring to the 'wave', which are conical in shape with sinuating sides and flat bottomed filter papers.

MELITTA

Another cone shaped filter method, with the differentiation here being a pinched draining point at the bottom of the cone rather than a point.

POUROVER

Manual brewing characterised by having a flow of fresh water through the bed of coffee, so you get a quicker, more aggressive extraction particularly around the outside of the ground coffee particle. Grind size must be spot on to get the best result.

SYPHON

This heats the water in an enclosed chamber using the resulting pressure to force the water into contact with the coffee in an upper chamber. When the heat's removed, the subsequent cooling then draws the coffee through a cloth filter back into the bottom chamber which is used to serve the coffee.

V60

Manufactured by Hario of Japan, this is the classic conical shaped brewer. It can be plastic, glass or ceramic, and all use the conical filter papers.

Jamie Treby

ESPRESSO

Given that cappuccinos, lattes, and a whole host of cafe drinks start as an espresso, this is an important brew method. However, espresso is subject to perhaps the widest variation of any style out there. Modern baristas will happily discuss brew ratios: the dry weight of the coffee 'in' to the wet weight of the liquid 'out' and use this to control quality. Traditionalists may still quote in terms of weight and time and volume of shot, so ask the barista – they should be able to talk about whatever method they choose.

MEET
THE COMMITTEE

JOHN THOMPSON

John owns Coffee Nexus, a coffee consultancy in Edinburgh. As well as working with numerous coffee roasters, brands and farmers across the UK and abroad, he's involved with the Speciality Coffee Association of Europe (SCAE) and helped develop its Coffee Diploma System. John's also written a manual for the Coffee Board of Malawi and is a head judge at the international Cup of Excellence.

LISA LAWSON

Lisa is a mover and shaker in the Scottish speciality coffee scene, and set up and runs Dear Green Coffee Roasters, the first roastery in Glasgow to only roast speciality coffee. She was also involved in the creation of Glasgow Coffee Festival and the Scottish AeroPress Championships. Lisa sources beans from across the globe and turns them into beautiful coffee which she supplies to cafes and direct to home baristas. *'We are committed to quality, flavour and a sustainable industry with ethical practices,'* she says.

DAVE LAW

Co-owner of Brew Lab, Dave Law hasn't always been a coffee connoisseur. Fresh out of uni he spent four years researching and developing the concept with co-founder Tom Hyde before opening the coffee bar and barista training ground in Edinburgh. He's been immersed in the industry ever since. When he's not working at the lab, you'll find Dave on his bike, playing music and visiting coffee shops around the world with his wife.

NICK COOPER

Nick is one of the founding directors at Salt Media, a boutique publishing, design and marketing company that hand crafts the *Indy Coffee Guides*. His obsession with coffee started 13 years ago when he was living and working in Sydney. A couple of barista courses and a lot of flat whites later, he and wife Jo returned to the UK with a serious plan to open an Aussie style coffee shop. They ended up creating Salt Media instead, so he gets his creative coffee kicks through his work on the guides.

INDEX

SCOTTISH
INDEPENDENT
COFFEE
GUIDE

№1